SARTRE

A BEGINNER'S GUIDE

GEORGE MYERSON

Hodder & Stoughton

A MEMBER OF THE HODDER HEADLINE GROUP

For the Rydin Myersons

Orders: please contact Bookpoint Ltd, 39 Milton Park, Abingdon, Oxon OX14 4TD. Telephone: (44) 01235 400400, Fax: (44) 01235 400500. Lines are open from 9.00–6.00, Monday to Saturday, with a 24-hour message answering service. Email address: orders@bookpoint.co.uk

British Library Cataloguing in Publication Data
A catalogue record for this title is available from The British Library

ISBN 0 340 78961 1

First published 2001
Impression number   10 9 8 7 6 5 4 3 2 1
Year   2005 2004 2003 2002 2001

Illustrations by Richard Chapman
Typeset by Transet Limited, Coventry, England.
Printed in Great Britain for Hodder & Stoughton Educational, a division of Hodder Headline Plc, 338 Euston Road, London NW1 3BH by Cox & Wyman, Reading, Berks

CONTENTS

Contents

Sartre's Life and Times

SARTRE'S WORLD

In Sartre's novel, *The Reprieve*, his central character, Mathieu Delarue has just listened to the voice of Adolf Hitler addressing the world on the radio. Although the war has been deferred it is nonetheless inevitable. Mathieu's thoughts filter into Sartre's own writing:

> A vast entity, a planet, in a space of a hundred million dimensions: three-dimensional beings could not so much as imagine it.
>
> *The Reprieve*

Each of those hundred million dimensions is a human 'consciousness': together, they make up this inconceivable planet, the earth.

Sartre was a major novelist and a leading dramatist. He was a central philosopher as well as a literary critic and biographer and produced a classic autobiography. Added to this, he founded several important periodicals and newspapers and was a distinguished journalist, as well as a travel writer and a political campaigner. Through all of these writings, and actions, this vision of the planet can be found: an earth which is different from every single human point of view, and yet which is also one shared place.

This image of the earth could also stand for Sartre's own work: a single whole which is also made up of a million different perspectives. To explore this unique world, we need to begin with this interweaving of Sartre's life, his writing and his century.

THE EARLY YEARS

Sartre himself has set the agenda for all stories of his early years through his autobiography, *Words*, written mainly in 1953 though not finally published until 1964. This strange book presents his childhood in a humorous and also philosophical way, and had such an impact that it provided the immediate cue for the offer to Sartre of the Nobel Prize for Literature (which he refused). Essentially, Sartre remembers himself as a false prodigy, who just happens, nevertheless, to have become the brilliant writer of this memoir and many other books. In interview with his chosen biographer, John Gerassi, Sartre summed up the irony of this childhood: 'surrounded by books, raised by books, I imagined myself more real in my books.'

Sartre File: The Early Years

- **1905** Jean-Paul-Charles-Aymand Sartre born in Paris on 21 July, son of Anne-Marie Schweitzer and Jean-Baptiste Sartre. His father died almost immediately.

- **1905–13** Brought up by his mother in the home of her father, Charles Schweitzer, an Alsatian teacher. Known as little 'Poulou', the prodigy did not go to school in his earlier years.

- **1913** Enrolled in the Lycée Montaigne, but fails to impress. Withdrawn from the school.

- **1914** The start of the First World War.

- **1915** Sent to school properly at Lycée Henri IV. Meets Paul Nizan, close friend at university and continuing rival in literature and politics.

- **1917** Anne-Marie marries the conservative businessman Joseph Mancy. She is 34, he is 43.

- **1918** The end of the First World War.

- **1919** Treaty of Versailles.

- **1920** Sartre returns to Lycée Henri IV as a boarder, and is under the care of his grandfather once more. Now reading serious contemporary writing, including Proust and Gide.

THE STUDENT, THE TEACHER AND THE YOUNG WRITER

Sartre's student career has also become famous, perhaps more through the memoirs of others, including his friend and lover Simone de Beauvoir. Highs and lows are well-chronicled, and it sets the tone for a certain idea of the Bohemian philosopher. Yet through it all, there runs an intense seriousness. His fellow philosophy student Raymond Aron told John Gerassi: 'He wanted a total change, without being a revolutionary', conjuring up a picture of intense, if frustrated, dedication. In the memory of Simone de Beauvoir, her first glimpse of Sartre in his room remained vivid: 'There were books all over the place, cigarette butts in all the corners, and the air was thick with tobacco smoke'.

Sartre File: The Student

- **1923** First published story, 'The Angel of Morbidity', *The Review Without Title*.

- **1924** Succeeds in exam to enter the elite *École Normale Supérieure*.

- **1924–8** Boarder and student at École. In class with Raymond Aron, Paul Nizan and above them Maurice Merleau-Ponty.

- **1927** Scandalous revue satire against French state.

- **1927** Early essay on what became his major philosophical concern – the nature of consciousness.

- **1928** Does poorly in competitive exams, claiming to be penalized by conventional examiners.

- **1929** First meeting with his lifelong companion, lover and collaborator Simone de Beauvoir, student at ENS.

- **1929** Comes first in this year's exams.

- **1929** 5 October, Wall Street Crash. Soon after French right comes to power under Tardieu and Laval.

The 1930s was, in retrospect, the decade leading to the Second World War: beginning with the Great Crash, through the rise of German Fascism and the Spanish Civil War. In France, the early part of the decade was dominated by Conservative governments. Later the left had more influence, but it was a decade of intense frustration for radicals and revolutionaries, typified by the refusal of the relatively liberal government of Leon Blum in 1936 to come to the aid of the Spanish republic against the right wing uprising led by General Franco and supported by Hitler and Mussolini. Sartre spent this decade first on military service and then as a teacher, with a spell in Berlin at precisely the time when Hitler came to power. Through it all, he was working on the book which became his first great success, the novel *Nausea*, and also on the philosophical ideas that were to become his famous Existentialism.

Sartre File: The Teacher and The Young Writer

- **1929** In November, Sartre begins 18 months military service.

- **1931** Takes up post as teacher in the town of Le Havre, the setting of his novel *Nausea*.

- **1931–3** Becomes teacher at Le Havre Lycée.

- **1933** March sees Hitler coming to power in Germany. Unrest in France. Sartre deepens his involvement with German philosophy from Hegel to Heidegger.

- **1933** Travels through Mussolini's Italy with De Beauvoir.

- **1933–4** Stays in Berlin.

- **1934** Still in Berlin on 30 June–1 July the Night of the Long Knives when Hitler disposes of right wing rivals. Composes second draft of novel to be published as *Nausea*.

- **1934–6** Returns to Le Havre to teach. De Beauvoir is in Rouen.

- **1935** Experiment with drug Mescalin goes awry compounding other strains to bring a period of extreme distress and even hallucination.

- **1936** Spanish Civil War. Popular Front comes to power in France.

- **1936–7** Teacher in Laon, north-east of Paris. De Beauvoir in Paris.

- **1936** In August publishes *Imagination* – a rewrite of an earlier essay on consciousness based on German philosophy, especially Husserl.

- **1937** Publishes story 'The Wall' in *Nouvelle Revue Francaise*.

- **1937** In April Daladier comes to power, with Conservative government.

- **1937** Sartre teaches at Lycée Pasteur in Paris.

- **1938** *Nausea* published by Gallimard. Nominated for Goncourt Prize and praised by Camus, Blanchot and others.

EXISTENTIALISM AT WAR

The period leading into the Second World War, and the French defeat by Nazi Germany, provided the subject matter for Sartre's greatest literary achievement, the trilogy *The Roads to Freedom*. The summer of 1938, as the Spanish Republic fell to Franco, was covered by the first novel *The Age of Reason*. The terrible September of 1938, sadly famous for the Munich agreement between Hitler, Daladier and Chamberlain ('Peace in our Time') became the subject of *The Reprieve*. The Second World War broke out on 1 September 1939, and Paris fell on 15 June 1940. The summer of 1940 is the subject matter for the third novel, *Iron in the Soul*. Sartre also wrote detailed diaries of the years 1939–40, which give vivid pictures of his life as a weather monitor in the army:

> The sky – my vertical dimension (because of the little balloons I send up there). Grey and motionless, with air currents whose curve can be traced.
>
> Monday 18 December 1939

> Minus 10 this morning. An antiseptic, charming cold ... Objects are smaller and sharper ...
>
> Saturday 23 December 1939

In these images are coiled many of the philosophical ideas of existentialism which Sartre was soon to make into a major influence on western thought and culture.

After the French surrender in June 1940, Sartre was a prisoner of war. He later managed to return to Paris and wrote several of his major works of philosophy and drama, notably the massive *Being and*

Nothingness, his most influential work as a philosopher, and the play *In Camera (No Exit)*. He was involved with the Resistance, and at the end of the war he wrote some of his most important journalism.

Sartre File: Existentialism at War

- **1939** On 1 September Germany invades Poland. On 2 September Sartre called up to act as a metereologist with artillery unit. Ten days later reports writing draft of *The Age of Reason*.

- **1940** *The Psychology of Imagination* expands and revises his treatment of human consciousness.

- **1940** On 23 May his close friend Paul Nizan is shot dead while acting as interpreter with British.

- **1940** Paris falls on 14 June. On 21 June Petain signs Armistice with the Germans and France falls. Sartre is taken prisoner to Stalag 12D near Trier in Germany.

- **1940–1** Writes 'almost a million and a half words' according to Gerassi. Finishes *The Age of Reason*; drafts much of *Being and Nothingness*, and writes and performs *Bariona*.

- **1941** In mid-March Sartre uses fake documents to leave camp and returns to Paris.

- **1941** Forms 'Socialism and Liberty' resistance group with De Beauvoir, Merleau-Ponty and others.

- **1941** In autumn, teaches at Lycée Condorcet in Paris.

- **1943** *Being and Nothingness* published by Gallimard. Meets Albert Camus who is organising the journal *Combat* and publishing works including *The Outsider* and *The Myth of Sisyphus*.

- **1943** Sartre's play *The Flies* opens in Paris, a pro-resistance work, part of changing climate as Allies begin to turn the war.

- **1944** 27 May – first performance of *In Camera (No Exit)*. Finishing drafts of *The Age of Reason* and *Iron in the Soul*.

- **1944** 22 August to 2 September contributes articles for *Combat* on fighting for the liberation of Paris and after.

- **1945** Publishes the first two volumes of *The Roads to Freedom*: *The Age of Reason* and *The Reprieve*. Announces there will be a sequel called *The Last Chance*.

- **1945** Refuses Legion d'Honneur from French government.

POST-WAR: THE HIGH TIDE OF INFLUENCE

In the years immediately after the Second World War, Sartre made himself into a symbol of a new era and was taken as such by many people. The term 'existentialism' became associated with his work and his ideas, and indeed his life, and stood for the hope that the new age would at last break free from the illusions of the past. However, Sartre himself entered a time of crisis by the early 1950s, and became increasingly involved in the political conflicts of the era, dominated by the rising Cold War between the West and the Soviet bloc. Sartre found himself associated with the cause of the Communist Party, though he never joined it formally. He became alienated from friends and colleagues, notably Albert Camus, over this political commitment. Though he launched an influential theory of fiction under the heading of 'committed writing', he himself abandoned the novel without completing the projected fourth and final book in the *Roads to Freedom*.

Sartre File: The High Tide of Influence

- **1945** First issue of Sartre's journal, *Modern Times* published in October. Committee includes de Beauvoir, Merleau-Ponty and Aron.

- **1945** Between January and June he visits the US and writes articles for *Combat* and *Le Figaro* on America. Meets President Roosevelt on 10 March.

- **1945** September sees the publication of De Beauvoir's *The Blood of Others*.

- **1945** On 24 October Sartre gives famous lecture in Brussels on existentialism, attended by Iris Murdoch. He has an even bigger audience on 28 Octoberat the Club Maintenant in Paris.

- **1947** Publishes *Situations I* to be followed by ten further collections.

- **1947** A series of theoretical essays entitled *What is Literature?* comes out in his journal *Modern Times*, from February to July. Statement of his philosophy of committed literature, engagement in current political struggles.

- **1948** Pope Pius XII bans all Sartre works for Catholics.

- **1948** USSR condemns a Finnish production of Sartre's play *Dirty Hands* saying it was 'hostile propaganda'.

- **1948** In July Sartre contributes to new journal, *La Gauche*, for movement for democratic revolution. Includes Camus and Merleau-Pony.

- **1948** Condemned as 'a hyena armed with a fountain pen' at conference of Russian Federation of Writers.

- **1949** Adds *Iron in the Soul* to *The Roads to Freedom* project instead of his earlier announced sequel.

- **1950** Divisions emerge on *Modern Times* over handling of Soviet labour camps. The start of split over Communist Party.

- **1952** Sartre finally abandons the project of *Roads to Freedom*, leaving off the planned fourth book, *The Last Chance*.

- **1952** In context of the Korean war, Sartre breaks off relations with Camus, Merleau-Ponty and others, taking a more anti-American path.

THE COLD WAR: MARXISM AND EXISTENTIALISM

After French Communist leaders were arrested and anti-American demonstrations were broken up, in 1952, Sartre began to work on a long essay series, 'The Communists and Peace', first appearing in July in *Modern Times*. This marked the start of a new phase of increasingly complex political thought and also engagement in current crises. In the first half of the 1950s Sartre was increasingly identified with the politics of the Communist Party. But there was a break in 1956, when the Soviet forces crushed an attempt to set up a more liberal version of socialism in Hungary. From then, Sartre moved away from his association with the Party and worked out an increasingly independent political outlook, culminating in his second major philosophical book, *The Critique of Dialectical Reason*, in which he tried to make his existential ideas the basis for a new approach to Marxism.

Sartre File: Marxism and Existentialism

- **1952** Publishes *Saint Genet.*
- **1953** 5 March – Death of Stalin.
- **1954** On 24 June Sartre visits Soviet Union for the first time.
- **1954** In December Sartre becomes vice-chair of Franco-Soviet Association.
- **1955** First visit to China.

- **1956** June sees risings in Poland and Hungary against Soviet power. October sees rising in Budapest. Soviet invasion of Hungary.

- **1956** On 7 November Sartre signs a letter with de Beauvoir condemning Soviet invasion. End of his co-operation with Communist Party.

- **1958** On 31 May Sartre meets the film director John Huston and agrees to write script for film on Freud. Never made.

- **1960** On 4 January Camus is killed in a car crash.

- **1960** In February Sartre goes to Cuba and meets Castro and Che Guevara.

- **1960** *The Critique of Dialectical Reason* (I) appears in May. Increasing association with politics of anti-colonial resistance. Writes preface for *The Wretched of the Earth* by Frantz Fanon.

INTO THE 1960s: THE RADICAL FATHER FIGURE

Throughout the 1960s, Sartre was associated with rising radical movements among students. These movements had new themes, notably the resistance to the Vietnam war, where US forces were involved in conflict between the communist North and the capitalist South. He was also associated with the anti-colonial uprising in Algeria against French rule, a position which had personal risks, since his flat in Paris was bombed twice by militant supporters of colonialism.

Sartre File: The Radical Father

- **1961** Flat bombed in July.

- **1962** Flat bombed in January.

- **1964** Sartre publishes the autobiographical *Words*.

- **1964** On 22 October Sartre is offered Nobel Prize for Literature. He rejects this Prize and provokes outrage in France. Condemned as Soviet propagandist.

- **1966** In November he gets involved in Bertrand Russell's Tribunal to condemn US 'war crimes' in Vietnam.

- **1967** In February he goes to Egypt and Israel, and Palestinian camps.

- **1968** Student demonstrations at Sorbonne in Paris on 3 May. On 6 May the unrest spreads. On 7 May 35,000 are on streets, including Sartre with a placard. By 11 May de Gaulle trying to negotiate. Riots night of 23 May after leader Cohn-Bendit is expelled from France. Sartre supports 'counter-violence'.

- **1969** Between 28 November and 1 December Sartre visits Prague in aftermath of liberal 'Prague spring'.

THE LAST YEARS

In the early 1970s, Sartre was increasingly involved with Maoist groups led by Alain Geismar and Benny Levy. Levy was to dominate Sartre's last years, once his sight failed. It is harder and harder to decide whose ideas one is hearing or reading, once Sartre's health began to fail in the early 1970s. Unable to read or write for himself, he depended on others, notably Levy, though he carried on playing an active public role.

Sartre File: The Last Years

- **1970** Associated with Maoist journal *La Cause du Peuple*.

- **1971** In May, publishes Part I of the massive life of Flaubert, *The Family Idiot*.

- **1973** Sartre closely involved with the first issue of new radical newspaper *Libération*.

- **1973** Sartre's health is failing and in December he loses his sight.

- **1974** Long interview with Michel Contat. Illness worse by October.

- **1977** In January, Sartre is hardly able to walk. Still involved in expressing support for prisoners on all sides.

- **1978–80** Sartre has apparently changed his main ideas, said to abandon revolution in both theory and practice, said to be reconciled with adversaries like the conservative thinker Raymond Aron.

- **1980** On 20 March Sartre collapses and is taken into hospital. He dies on 15 April.

- **1980** 19 April 50,000 people follow Sartre's coffin.

PLAN OF THE GUIDE

Dates were always important to Sartre. He attached specific times to many of his writings, including much of the fiction and drama. He founded a journal entitled *Modern Times* to chronicle the changing era. The theme of his more abstract philosophy was often the passing of time and the present moment, whether for the individual or for a society. In this guide, I have followed this basic principle of Sartre's work and have arranged the sequence of chapters in relation to Sartre's own significant dates.

2 Evening in a Municipal Park, 1932: Existence and the Lone Individual

NAUSEA

Sartre's fame began with a novel called *Nausea*, which he published in 1938 having worked on it since 1931. In this chapter, we will look at this novel and its central moment, in which Sartre dramatizes an idea which became the basis of his philosophical development, the idea of existence, and specifically of the lone individual upon whose consciousness this 'existence' suddenly bursts with terrifying force.

AN EXISTENTIAL HERO: ANTOINE ROQUENTIN

Nausea presents some experiences of a character called Antoine Roquentin, in his own words. A note at the start tells us that the 'editors' have decided to publish a journal found among Roquentin' s papers, the author himself having disappeared, maybe travelling or, it seems, perhaps dead. On the face of it, not much happens in this journal. The writer seems to feel afflicted by a strange condition which he calls 'the nausea', and his diary is mainly about the threat and onset of this weird state.

So who is Roquentin and why is he the medium through which Sartre expresses his deepest philosophical concerns?

Character File: Antoine Roquentin

- Antoine Roquentin was 30 years old at the time of his journal, which was written between Monday 29 January 1932 and a Wednesday later on that spring.

- He lived in a hotel in provincial Bouville (Mudville), where he wrote a history book about the Marquis de Rollebon, a sinister eighteenth-century aristocrat whose papers were in the town library.

- He travelled widely and used much of his money. At the time he had an income of 14,400 francs per year, enough to live very moderately.

- Apart from casual liaisons, his one important relationship was with Anny, with whom he was obsessesed and who was now being kept by an older man.

In *Nausea*, Sartre explores the world through the consciousness of this lonely man, who lives entirely in the impersonal spaces of a town which belongs to others. We follow Roquentin in his own journal entries, from his hotel room to the Café Mably, and from there to the town library. We see the town streets through which he walks, including the posh parade of a bourgeois Sunday, and the shabby dark of the downtown night. Only two individuals really enter this drifting consciousness. One is Anny, who has written to say she is arriving, and whom Roquentin is waiting to meet at her hotel. The other is a pathetic figure called only 'the Autodidact', a man who is trying to read through the library, book by book, in alphabetical order.

Roquentin's early journal entries sometimes have precise dates, beginning on Monday 29 January 1932. The key theme of the book is announced in a section heading '5.30' on a day which is dated previously as Friday, 2 February:

Things are very bad: I've got it, that filthy thing, the Nausea

Throughout the diary, Roquentin struggles with his terror at the onset of this nausea.

From café, to street, to art gallery, Roquentin flees this feeling, looking out for safe places, where his personal life can merge with the surroundings. However, he fails, and the crisis deepens. Roquentin has met the Autodidact, the self-educator, for lunch, from which he has rushed in disgusted panic. He writes, 'all of a sudden, there it is: the nausea.'

Concept File: *The Nausea*

- Nausea is a reaction to the world itself. The world is unbearable, as a fact by which one is surrounded.

- Nausea is the opposite of madness, in the sense that it involves too strong a sensation of reality, rather than a loss of reality.

- Nausea is an over-consciousness of *existence*. In nausea, everything stands out in harsh clarity: 'Now I know, I exist, the world exists'.

- Nausea involves a feeling of absurdity, things existing for no reason, including oneself.

After the nausea, Roquentin is ready for his crisis in the park.

KEY MOMENT: THE MUNICIPAL PARK – EVENING, 1932

The nausea has set in. In a few days, Roquentin will see Anny, who is passing through Bouville. We reach a journal entry headed 'Six o'clock in the evening', which has been written immediately after an experience in the local park. No date is given, unlike earlier in the text. The days have become too empty for particular dates.

What we are now reading is meant to be a journal entry composed by Roquentin just after his experience. But the effect is that of immediacy. The moment begins with everyday life. Roquentin reports that he has just come back from the park. Evidently, he went there as a refuge from the terrible feeling. He went to put his isolation in a public setting, as if the park might rescue him. Might he not become just another person, any other person, like all those blurred passing presences you see as you walk down the road?

Roquentin pictures himself sitting alone. He has no purpose, except his flight from nausea. All he does to the world is look. He sees a chestnut tree, an experience originally recorded in a Sartre letter of 1931; one which it took him a long time to digest, though in the novel Roquentin takes only minutes. Antoine remembers how his gaze zooms in on the tree's complex root, folded at his feet. He records the experience as if seeing overcame all his powers of remembering. He could not even recall the word for this thing on which his look had fallen:

> The root of the chestnut tree plunged into the ground just underneath my bench. I no longer remembered that it was a root.

Words identify the world as we look around. Usually, as adults at least, we have a kind of automatic commentary which accompanies our roaming look. As a result, what we see always seems to consist not of 'things', but of thises and thats – entities which belong to recognisable types. I see not just objects, but tables or trees. When names fail him, Roquentin has a moment of pure seeing, and in that moment his gaze falls upon existence itself, unshared with anyone else, beyond community or communication.

Roquentin's experience provided Sartre with an opportunity to define his idea of existence.

Concept File: Existence

- **The Inexplicable.** Existence is the quality of the world insofar as we can neither classify things nor explain them. Roquentin says that the chestnut root 'existed in so far as I could not explain it'.

- **The Pointless.** We normally ignore this brute existence. Our main way of doing this is by having a purpose in our dealings with the world. As Roquentin says, things normally 'served me as tools', but here have no purpose.

At the heart of what we will be exploring as Sartre's existentialism there is this fearful encounter with the world.

Roquentin has lost the names for these objects around him. But in his diary, he then finds a new word to define how things exist, without saying what they are: 'Absurdity'. The absurd is a major concept in twentieth-century philosophy, literature and art.

Concept File: The Absurd

- The absurd is a term for the ways in which the world defies human efforts to find coherent meaning.

- Absurdity arises from the fact that things, including people, co-exist without being connected.

- The absurd was originally a concept used by Christian thinkers, who had argued that the basis of faith was absurdity. For Sartre, this lack of reasons becomes an argument for atheism instead.

- Other major writers associated with 'the absurd' include Camus, Ionesco and Beckett.

With these glimpses of the absurd, the novel has reached its climax. Briefly, the characters are disposed of. The poor Autodidact is expelled from the library where he has been seen fondling a boy's hand. Roquentin seems now capable of more genuine fellow-feeling, but he can do nothing to comfort. The meeting with Anny passes without contact. Roquentin abandons his history book, and disappears. We are left with his journal of nausea.

SARTRE'S EARLY PHILOSOPHY: CONTEXTS

During the years he was writing *Nausea*, Sartre was exploring the questions posed by some leading thinkers of the time. He was particularly engaged by the ideas of two German philosophers, Edmond Husserl and Martin Heidegger.

Concept File: Husserl and Phenomenology

- Edmond Husserl was a leading German philosopher in the period during and after the Great War of 1914–18.

- His approach is known as Phenomenology, which means 'the science of the thing'. This approach influenced many twentieth-century thinkers, in the social sciences, literary criticism, art and philosophy.

- At the centre of Husserl's thought is the idea of 'consciousness'. He analysed our experience in terms of how this consciousness projects its intentions.

It was this 'science of the thing' to which Sartre responded when he created the moment in the park through Roquentin. Sartre also set out his response to phenomenology in a book called *The Psychology of The Imagination*, published in 1940. Here he set out to understand how things exist for our consciousness: not what they are, just how they exist, and how we experience their existence.

His ideas help further in explaining the nausea, though the philosophy itself has not the same dark tone. First, Sartre found that things exist all together. There is a going-together about them. In the past, western thought had discerned a kind of unity about the world, sometimes called God or Reason or Meaning. But for Sartre, the way things exist together has no basis beyond them. It is simply the case that 'every "thing" has an infinite number of relationships to other things'. The tree's curling root can be seen as a metaphor for this coiled connection between things. Using the approach of Husserl, Sartre looked at how these things make a world. At every moment, we face what he calls 'the overflowing in the world of things', as each coils into the other in a network that extends far beyond our grasp.

Husserl raised for Sartre the question of things, and how they become worlds. But what about the dark tone of Sartre's approach? In part, that is Sartre's personal feeling. However, it is also coloured by the thought of the second German thinker, Martin Heidegger.

Concept File: Heidegger and Anxiety

- Martin Heidegger's major work, *Being and Time*, came out in 1927, and was dedicated to Husserl.

- Heidegger asked how people relate to things and to the world. The usual way is to have a purpose for which we use things. We then have 'dealings with equipment' and that equipment makes up the world.

- If we don't turn everything into 'equipment', we have instead what Heidegger calls 'just looking'. This is where we confront directly 'the phenomenon of the world'.

- Just looking isn't a peaceful experience. When you really encounter 'the world as such', you do so with '*anxiety*'.

Roquentin's moment in the park condenses many key ideas from Husserl and Heidegger, as re-imagined by the young Sartre as he reached towards his own personal vision.

A Paris Café, Summer 1938: Inauthentic Living and 'The Other'

THE AGE OF REASON

We have seen how Sartre begins with the lone individual faced by existence. But even in the earliest work, he is already aware of the problem of other people's existence. As his thought and fiction develop, Sartre becomes increasingly concerned to reconcile two truths: the truth that each individual is alone; and the truth that we have no sense of our own being which does not involve others.

In this chapter, we shall see how Sartre deepens his idea of the individual and the other in his major novel, *The Age of Reason*. This work was published in 1945, after the liberation of France from Nazi rule. However, the setting is pre-war Paris in 1938, and most of the writing was done in the early years of the war. Indeed Sartre wrote parts of this novel while a prisoner of war after the German victory in 1940. The book is self-standing but also the first volume of the famous trilogy entitled *The Roads to Freedom*, which will be considered further in the next two chapters.

PHILOSOPHICAL CONTEXT: THE BASIC CHOICE OF LIFE

Like *Nausea*, this fiction makes most sense when taken together with the philosophical writings of the same period. As a thinker, Sartre was struggling to come up with a language that could define human existence. Starting with the truth of individuality, he sought a deeper understanding of how 'others' enter our lives. For our reading of *The Age of Reason*, two concepts are important. First, there is Sartre's attempt to define the different ways in which a person can respond to his or her own individuality. The key concept here is *inauthenticity*, which Sartre developed in response to ideas he found in Heidegger. His general definition was worked out in *Being and Nothingness* at the same time as he was finalising *The Age of Reason*.

Concept File: Inauthenticity

- We have a basic *choice* in life. We can choose to be *authentic* or *inauthentic*.

- To be *authentic* means to experience fully the fact of your own unique being.

- To be *inauthentic* means to try to escape your own individuality, to live as if you were not a distinct person. Sartre calls this 'the inauthentic mode of "the they"'.

- Much of everyday life is inauthentic. Sartre gives as examples of 'inauthentic possibilities' everything which as a person you share with 'everybody': mass-produced clothes, buses and trains, public parks, public places, public shelters.

Essentially, I am living an inauthentic life when I experience myself as if I were just one of the 'others'. I go where 'everybody' goes. I choose things not as 'me' but as one of 'the they'. These choices are their choices: my clothes, my pattern of commuting to work and back, my drink in the bar.

Closely connected to inauthenticity is Sartre's concept of 'The Other'. You might think that other people belong to the outside world which each person encounters as the scene of his life. Sartre introduces into his language an idea of 'the Other' as a part of the inner world.

Concept File: The Other

- 'The Other' is a term for a general presence, an aspect of how each person experiences not only the world, but also their own being.

- 'The Other' is part of 'my' consciousness. I have no way of being aware of who I am without some sense of how I appear from another point of view. Sartre defines 'the Other' as a 'mediator between myself and me'.

- The most graphic example of 'the Other' is 'Shame'. Sartre uses 'shame' to define this otherness inside us all. As he says, *I am ashamed of myself as I appear to 'the Other'*. To feel ashamed of myself, I have to view my life from an alien perspective.

Inauthentic living is an escape from both 'I' and 'Other', into a soothing third person experience.

MATHIEU DELARUE: A FREE MAN?

Let us now turn to *The Age of Reason*. The central character is Mathieu Delarue, who will continue as a major figure in *The Roads to Freedom* trilogy.

Character File: Mathieu Delarue

- At the start of the story, in the summer of 1938, Mathieu is a 35-year-old philosophy teacher at the Lycée Buffon in Paris, with a few published stories.

- Mathieu hasn't married, to the annoyance of his respectable lawyer brother, Jacques. He has a long-standing commitment to his lover Marcelle, and at the same time he pursues the younger Ivich, a Russian student in Paris.

- Mathieu is the philosophical voice for Sartre's struggle with the idea of individuality and inauthenticity. His central aim in life is to stay true to his own 'freedom'.

At the start of novel, Marcelle tells Mathieu that she is pregnant. Stunned and also appalled, he presumes that the thing to do will be to arrange an abortion, currently illegal. She appears to consent, and so he leaves the stuffy room where she lives, like an invalid, an almost housebound life. This is the summer night, 1938, which Sartre uses to develop his key concepts of Inauthenticity and the Other.

KEY MOMENT: A PARIS CAFÉ, SUMMER EVENING, 1938

In the dark street, Mathieu thinks he feels relief. He has escaped. And what he has escaped, it seems, is his lover's gaze: 'she was no longer looking at him'. Only now, he feels, can he be truly himself, 'alone'. Then comes a revelation, which is equivalent to the moment in the park for Roquentin. Mathieu's revelation is about 'the Other'. He realises abruptly that his comforting isolation 'wasn't true', 'he wasn't alone', and indeed it seems he can never be alone. He feels the presence of Marcelle. But it is not just the idea of his lover which displaces the charm of being alone. It is the thought that she is thinking about him which is the poison:

She was thinking of him …

It is a nightmare moment, and one to which Sartre returns in his plays as well as his fiction.

As we have seen, Sartre defines 'the Other' as a mediator between myself and me. This scene helps explain the idea. Mathieu is trying to recover his sense of himself, who he is. But his thoughts come back to him being coloured by this feeling of being seen from outside. Marcelle has come to embody 'the Other' in whom Mathieu finds his identity reinterpreted. There is no thought of Mathieu apart from this Other. 'Shame' is a good term for the experience: shame is to Mathieu what the nausea was to Antoine.

Roquentin spent his time fleeing nausea. He knew he was doomed when the feeling followed him even into his café, which had been a refuge because, in Sartre's developing philosophy, it was a place which belonged to him only as one of 'everybody' else. Mathieu, too, is in flight, and he sees a café across the street. The scene is a systematic example of inauthentic living. First, Mathieu sees a man he recognizes only as 'the landlord', in other words, a type and not an individual, a role that could be performed by anybody. This anonymous figure is stacking the chairs. Anybody could do this task: it is a symbol of the world of 'the they'. The chairs are public furniture. They belong to everyone and no one, and they are piled up in a heap which emphasizes how they are identical, featureless. In this bar, even the objects lack identity. Everything is interchangeable. Later we will see how Sartre developed a concept called 'seriality', list-like being, to define this kind of existence.

Mathieu enters. He needs 'to be seen', because then he can escape from Marcelle, the Other inside, the gaze which is really tormenting him. Mathieu opens the door and walks in – like anyone and everyone else who enters. The act belongs to every customer equally. When you go through that door, you cease to exist as Mathieu the individual and become Mathieu the customer. He props his elbows on the bar: again, the place and posture belong to him as customer, not as individual. He is performing inauthenticity.

It is not just acts that can be inauthentic. So can words. Mathieu speaks: 'Good evening, everybody'. These kinds of phrase belong to us insofar as we are any speaker of the language. You can't tell one person from another in such a phrase. Mathieu chooses to behave inauthentically, as 'everybody', because he is escaping his own consciousness of himself, a consciousness at whose heart is the critical presence of Marcelle.

In the bar, Mathieu is seeking to place himself in front of a different kind of Other. He wants to replace the intimate, hostile look of his lover with the cool, empty otherness of the landlord and the customers. These people care nothing about him as an individual. In their eyes, he is just one of the boys, a causal sharer of the public space. He looks at the landlord and a man who exists for him only as a beer-drinking 'bus conductor'. They are 'kindly, casual consciousnesses'. In their presence, he finds that his 'consciousness released him'.

The conversation could be anyone talking anywhere: 'You're quite a stranger', 'It's thirsty weather'. The landlord cleans, the conductor whistles. Everything and every person is shrouded in a kind of haze of generality. Philosophically, you could say that the 'existence' of these objects and people is muted, they don't thrust themselves upon Mathieu. Therefore, he can see himself in the same way: hazily, in a general sort of fashion, as a nice chap like the others. He 'felt at ease'. The scene is a classic analysis of what it means to be inauthentic and why people make that choice.

THE AGE OF REASON: AN OVERVIEW

Mathieu sets off to find money to pay for Marcelle's abortion. At the same time, he falls in love with Ivich, a young Russian student. His journey takes him into a sequence of encounters, in each of which he tries to be authentic, and fails. For example, he reaches out to embrace Ivich in a taxi. For an instant, the act seems real, a free and spontaneous moment of true feeling: 'This time, it was love.' But soon, Mathieu is thinking, and he is aware of how he must look to Ivich. He is lost in the labyrinth of 'The Other': 'she would think him like the rest'. His consciousness is taken over by anxiety, about how he must be being thought about. In other words, Mathieu is worrying about seeming inauthentic, when a while ago in the bar he was relieved by the same feeling. This is the trap of modern life, as seen by Sartre in philosophy and the novel. We want to escape into the world of 'everybody', until at certain moments we wish to come back to our own unique being. But there is no way back.

The Age of Reason is a lasting vision of modern urban life. In another bar scene, Ivich is sitting with Mathieu and her brother Boris. She picks up a knife and stabs her own hand, in a gesture directed at the indignant gaze of a lady from the next door table. Mathieu responds by copying her: '... anybody can do that.' These people rob each other of every vestige of authenticity. They envy every moment of free action or even apparent spontaneity. In a tangle of plotting, Mathieu steals some money from the room of Lola, who is Boris's older lover. He thinks he is about to be exposed when Lola bursts into his flat, where he is trying to persuade Ivich to take the money and stay in Paris. Then the money reappears, in the hands of the manipulative Daniel, who also marries Marcelle and takes on the baby. Mathieu rages to Daniel that, 'All I do, I do for nothing': he feels his actions have no effect. Their consequences are 'stolen' from him. Nothing he does belongs to him, as an individual. These people have stolen from each other their authentic possibilities. In envy and bitterness, in fear and anger, they rob one another of everything free or personal. In each other's eyes, each is empty of their own true humanity.

4 Monday, 26 September 1938: Hitler on the Radio

THE REPRIEVE: THE FUTURES OF SEPTEMBER 1938

This chapter takes its cue from Sartre's novel *The Reprieve*, second in the *Roads to Freedom* trilogy, and written after France had fallen to the Germans. This book is Sartre's exploration of what having a future means, and what it meant in the world just before the war came. What meaning do our old futures have, once they have become part of the past themselves?

The novel is also Sartre's exploration of a moment, the episode which is now known as the Munich crisis, when the British and French leaders made a final attempt to negotiate with Hitler, and prevent the outbreak of the Second World War. On 21 April 1938, Hitler was preparing to invade Czechoslovakia. There was a respite, and on 15th September the British Prime Minister, Chamberlain, and the French President, Daladier, held their notorious meeting at Berchtesgaden with Hitler. Chamberlain famously came home brandishing his 'piece of paper' which guaranteed, he said, 'Peace in Our Time'. Two weeks later Czechoslovakia fell.

Set at this moment of heightened anticipation, *The Reprieve* jumps rapidly from one character to another, one place to another, around Europe as everyone is waiting to learn whether war has been avoided. Mathieu Delarue appears as just one among these many viewpoints, as he waits with his brother Jacques and sister-in-law Odette, in the south of France. Mathieu is going to be called up and, during the novel, the notices summoning all the reserves are pasted on the walls. His time is coming.

The same seems to be true for each character. In Czechoslovakia, Milan and Anna are listening anxiously to the radio. They are Czechs, but outside, the local German population is marching in support of Hitler's takeover of their country. The talks are about them and their future, or lack of a future. A young man called Philippe is running away from his military stepfather, and trying to live up to his pacifist ideals: he ends up innocently asleep in a brothel. M. Birnenschatz, the Jewish-French businessman, is insisting to himself and others on his Frenchness.

You can map the world in terms of futures as they exist for each person at that moment in time, and history, as Hitler speaks.

Character Files: September 1938

Character	Position	Future	Key Quote
Mathieu (French)	Teacher; unmarried	Army	'He was leaving his life behind: I have cast my skin.'
Daniel (French)	Financier; married to Marcelle; homosexual	Blank	'Oh God, if only war would come.'
Milan (Czech)	Teacher	Exile, death	'The voices seemed nearer: they must be marching down the main street.'
Brunet (French)	Communist	Political	'...to protect their slow tenacious minds against all the bastards who try to muck up their thinking.'
M. Birnenschatz and father (French/Jew)	Businessman	Concentration camp	'Race? – what do you mean by race?'
Jacques Delarue (French)	Lawyer; patriarch	Survival	'I know you don't like the Hitler regime.'

The novel imitates a journal, though unlike *Nausea* it is no one's diary. Each day is experienced by a succession of isolated consciousnesses. You can feel these people living simultaneously, yet separately. On the same day, 24 September 1938, Mathieu is thinking of sending a letter to Ivich and how she will react. M. Birnenschatz is trying not to think about his future as a French Jew. Gomez, a veteran of the Spanish Civil War, is thinking about fighting the fascists again and finally winning. His wife, Sarah, is thinking about herself as a refugee carrying the corpse of their small son, Pablo. Georges is looking at his small daughter and thinking of a future which will not happen: 'She was just beginning to love me.' Daniel is dreaming of a great war which will end the life in which he is trapped.

The novel comes to a climax in a chapter dated 'Monday, 26 September', when Hitler's speech to a Nazi rally is relayed over the radio. It seems he has rejected the deal offered by Britain and France. War has come. But this future turns out to be false: the deal is patched together again. But then again, the peace is false, and the war will come, a little later. The reprieve is temporary. The novel makes you ask a question, one which Sartre also expressed in his philosophical work, *Being and Nothingness*:

And what type of being does the future possess?

SARTRE'S FUTURES

Before we look at the key moment, when the world listens as Hitler speaks, let us examine what the future meant in Sartre's philosophy at that time. Sartre is interested in the future as it exists for the present. What, he wants to know, does it tell us about our experience of the present that it includes all kinds of futures?

The usual way to think about the present and the future is to ask: Does this 'future' come true? But Sartre turns the problem around. By definition, a future is always an elsewhere. For example, he says in *Being and Nothingness*, I look up at the moon, and what I see is a crescent shape. In effect, I am seeing the present moon as an incomplete circle in the sky. What's missing is precisely the future of this image, the missing arc of the circle:

The full moon is future…

But that future is only 'there' from my human point of view. The future is a missing aspect of the present world as experienced by a human being. The future, says Sartre, is another name for what we feel is needed to complete the present:

…it is only by human reality that the Future arrives in the world.

From the point of view of many people in September 1938, the name for the incompleteness of the present time was the next war. The date 24 September 1938 was like a crescent moon whose missing arc was the declaration of war. For each person that missing portion looks different. For M. Birnenschatz it is being tortured to death in a camp; for Milan in his small town in Czechoslovakia it is the stone which is about to smash through his window; for Daniel, it is a cleansing apocalypse.

However, there are also lots of everyday futures. One example Sartre gives is playing tennis. He is running in to the net and bending forwards with his racquet to return the ball. If you froze the posture it would make no sense except 'through the movement which I shall make immediately afterward with my racket in order to return the ball over the net'. In other words, the present stance is as incomplete as the crescent in the sky. The missing portion now is the movement by which he will complete the stroke.

KEY MOMENT: MONDAY, 26 SEPTEMBER 1938 AT 8.30 P.M.

On a train heading towards the army, Mathieu keeps checking the time: he is waiting for something. Like everyone else, he knows that Hitler is about to broadcast his speech: 'In ten minutes Hitler is going to speak.' That broadcast is a missing portion of the present, and it's not only Mathieu who sees the moment as having what Sartre calls this 'trajectory'. Like the train, the present is heading towards Hitler on the radio. What everyone thinks is that this speech will be the start of the true future, the war, which will complete all the present moments that have made up the time now called the 'interwar' period, since 1918.

Meanwhile, Mathieu's brother Jacques is tuning his radio set in the living room:

> 'Are you sure you've got Stuttgart?' asked Odette.
> 'Hush –' said Jacques. 'Yes, I'm sure.'

This conversation creates a present moment which is incomplete in the same way as Mathieu's experience. This room is deficient, from the point of view of its inhabitants, because it lacks the sound of Hitler on the radio. The radio speech becomes a missing part of the world, a gap waiting to be filled.

The set tunes in and suddenly the voice begins to speak. For an instant, we are at the rally, where Hitler raises his right arm, and then we are given the words, as they come over on the air across Europe:

> Fellow citizens, there is a limit …

The old moon is complete, the gap has been filled or, to put it less philosophically, the waiting is over: ' "Here he is" says Jacques.' Though the words are banal, there is a profound idea behind them, an idea of which Jacques is not really aware. Suddenly, and temporarily, all these people feel a sense of completeness: something has come about, as a result of which their experience feels finished.

But the completeness is extremely brief, perhaps just momentary. This is the nature of the human experience of the future, in Sartre's terms. What is happening in this vivid episode represents a general truth about the human condition, as well as an account of a key moment in western and world history. As they listen, each person in the audience is asking: What is he going to say next? Is he going to declare war now? To pick up Sartre's philosophical analysis again, this moment shows that the future is always the 'beyond' of the present.

If you wanted to select one passage to stand for the uniqueness of Jean-Paul Sartre's contribution to western thought, 'Monday, 26 September 1938' would be a good choice. We are given in turn a series of experiences as people listen to Hitler on the radio. There is Mathieu, for whom the moment is a kind of annihilation of all his efforts, lifelong efforts, to be rational about the world:

> *He speaks!* Mathieu made a violent effort to hear him, then he suddenly felt hollow, and switched his mind off.

He confronts a future where this pure voice, 'he speaks', will make all thinking impossible.

Then there is M. Birnenschatz who begins to talk back to the voice, so angry and frightened is he:

> The wireless shouted: "Shame! Shame!" and M.Birnenschatz exlaimed: "Liar! Those Germans were not taken from Germany!"

In a later work, *The Critique of Dialectical Reason*, which we shall consider more fully in Chapters 10 and 11 especially, Sartre returned to this kind of behaviour among radio audiences: 'In fact, I feel as though I could challenge the arguments put forward by this voice.' But as a listener, you cannot actually challenge the voice: no one else will hear you, no one will count your response. You are drawn into a kind of illusory dialogue, in which you win a debate that can never actually occur. We all still do this, as media audiences. We all know just how to win the argument against this repellent speaker to whom we still go on listening. Our winning reply belongs to an alternative future, one which can never happen, and which serves only to keep us trapped in the unfolding present as passive listeners.

Ella, Birnenschatz's daughter, listens to Hitler and has a different experience again. First she wants to stop listening: 'We don't have to listen', she thinks angrily. Then she feels as if the voice on the radio has filled up the world, it was 'there, enormous', all around her. Finally she experiences absolute isolation, being alone in the world with that voice. Ella is experiencing a future which is no future: her world has come to a stop with these words.

Here we reach a paradox in Sartre's philosophy of the future. We have a sense of futures only because our world feels incomplete. Surely it would be good to experience completion, a world that was finally present once and for all? This episode shows that nothing could be worse, from Sartre's point of view, than such an experience of the world. When Hitler speaks, the world seems to be absolutely finished for many people listening. The future has ended, and with it has gone all possibility: the future is a gap in the present, but without that gap we are no longer free.

18 June 1940 at 6.00 a.m. – 5
A French Village Square:
Modern Times

IRON IN THE SOUL

Iron in the Soul is the third novel in the *Roads to Freedom* trilogy. Here Sartre tells the story of the French defeat, as experienced by different characters in varied circumstances. But they all have one thing in common: the time. Gomez is a refugee in New York, having been a General on the losing side in the Spanish Civil War. His Jewish wife, Sarah, and their small son Pablo, are trying to escape from Paris. Mathieu is with his fellow soldiers in the now redundant French army. Daniel is roaming the streets of Paris, waiting for the Germans to come. Different places, different feelings, different lives: but they all belong to the time. For all these people, on 15 June 1940, a new world began – a world after the defeat of France.

The novel has two parts. Part I is arranged like a diary, from Saturday, 15 June to Tuesday, 18 June, often with specific hours and even minutes. Unlike *Nausea*, this is not the journal of an individual: there is no 'narrator', no 'I' to link these moments into a single record. In the first section, 15 June, we move from Gomez in New York, at nine and ten o'clock in the morning, to Sarah for whom it is three o'clock in the French afternoon. The point is to show that people share time in a much more profound sense than merely setting their watches together. These characters belong to a moment together, whether they are aware of the connection or not. Sartre uses the diary form to present his ideas of time itself, while also analysing the occasion of France's shame and Europe's calamity – the fall of Paris. At the centre of the novel, there is a key moment, when Mathieu stakes his life at last on a single act – in a French village square at six o'clock in the morning. But this moment of action is connected with Sartre's whole interpretation of modern times.

SARTRE'S MODERN TIMES

After the war, Sartre edited a journal which was called *Modern Times*.
Here, he explores the meaning of time for human beings in certain
modern predicaments, which have come to symbolize the dark sides of
the world we still inhabit.

Character File: *Iron in the Soul*

Modern condition	Character	Experience of time	Date in history
Refugee	Gomez, Sarah	Infinite present	15 June 1940, fall of Paris
Redundant crowd	Mathieu, French soldiers	Frozen moments	16 June 1940, after the fall
Impotent patriarch	Jacques, Daniel	Strategic future	17 June 1940, arrival of the Germans
Protestor	Mathieu	Free time	18 June 1940,

Here are four negative conditions which cover a great deal of modern
history. Sartre shows how characters' lives fall into these patterns, as the
city surrenders. In many ways, we have two pairs of complementary
opposites. The *refugees* have to keep on moving, whereas the *redundant*
crowd have to sit still and wait for nothing. On the one side, there is
frantic desperation; on the other side, empty passivity. The little
patriarchs aim to stay on top of their small worlds, and to fit in with the
new order; the *protestor* looks for one last gesture of defiance, one final
refusal to fit in.

These lives are different in space. For the refugees, the world is vast and
crowded; for the protestor, space shrinks to the context of one last
action. What about time?

On 15 June 1940, time is like this for Gomez:

REFUGEE TIME: THE EXILE
'Ten o'clock in Paris. Livid and hopeless, the afternoon lay hidden behind this Colonial morning.'

Gomez is the refugee in exile, and for him time is 'hidden'. Really, it is afternoon, Paris time; but he is stuck in the American morning. Split into two time zones, he feels the present as an endless expanse, 'livid and hopeless'. His wife, Sarah, is a different refugee, one of the columns who have walked through so many modern disasters and defeats, carrying their children as they go:

REFUGEE TIME: THE FUGITIVE
'She must start once more to live; start once more to walk.'

We tend to think of refugees in spatial terms: arriving here, fleeing there. But Sartre sees the condition in time: as an experience of an infinite and unbounded present tense, the time of endless walking.

On 16 June, the day after the fall, time is different for Mathieu as he sits on the grass with the other soldiers, waiting for the Germans to come and round them up:

REDUNDANT TIME
'Sunday 16 June. The Germans are in Paris and we have lost the war. Another morning, another beginning. The world's first morning: precisely like every other morning: everything waiting to be done: all the future in the sky.'

Their future is a pure series of identical days, morning after morning, each a new beginning, each going nowhere. In his philosophy, Sartre calls such a condition 'exteriority', a standing outside one's own life as it moves by. In *Being and Nothingness*, he talks vividly of an experience for which 'this future is a series of empty containers'. Redundant time moves forward but is 'composed of "nows" each one indifferent to the others'. As a result, for the aimless mob the moment is frozen solid. There is no sense of what Sartre calls 'trajectory'.

Elsewhere, others are directing more active efforts towards the future. On one side are the little, lost patriarchs. These characters live their lives by dominating those immediately around them. One such is Jacques, Mathieu's brother. He is driving with his wife Odette through the south, and every moment is still filled with little strategies and commands:

PATRIARCHAL TIME
'We're going to sleep here.'

He has a future, but it is only a small space, filled with little moves and contrivances. He is already accommodating to the Nazi order, the new era. Then there is Daniel, the gay man, who finds a new subordinate on the streets of Paris, the lost boy, Philippe, pacifist son of a general. For Daniel, a different kind of patriarch, the future is also planned out as a strategy for maintaining his personal dominion. He looks up at the Nazi flag and sees 'the Monogram of Evil, my monogram'.

The patriarchs experience the future in terms of master-slave relationships. They will submit to the big power, in return for preserving their small dominions. Finally, there is the future of the protestor, or the one who resists. By 19 June, Mathieu has joined a small group of fighters. They are waiting for the German army to reach their village, and then they are going to open fire, kill and, presumably, die. This is the time of 'the protestor'.

KEY MOMENT: 18 JUNE 1940 AT 6.00 A.M. – A FRENCH VILLAGE SQUARE

Mathieu looks out from his vantage point over the village square. He sees a world moving *towards* a future: 'the road made a bend to the west … Mathieu could make out a number of motor vehicles …'. The road is like time itself, as experienced by someone in Mathieu's position, on the verge of a last, significant gesture. You can feel the bend in the road, as if just around the corner the future was approaching. There is a 'trajectory' to time, as to space: the future is being reborn.

All objects are filled with this feeling of moving 'towards'. On the horizon, he can just make out the vehicles, but he knows soon they will be in focus. That feeling brings with it all kinds of other images. Mathieu immediately has the strange thought that these Germans, who are coming towards him, will be the ones to see his dead body. So Mathieu experiences even his own body as having a trajectory, a direction. This feeling of 'towards-ness' is different from the sense of time as encountered by all the other conditions we have covered. For the refugee, there is no horizon; for the redundant mob, there is no movement at all; for the patriarchs, there is a small, threatening space which they struggle to control. But for Mathieu now, the future is dynamic, a different world coming towards him, and towards which he is advancing.

Every object is now incomplete, like the crescent moon in the night sky. When Mathieu sees 'two motor cyclists, dressed in black …', he is also watching the approach of the moment when he will open fire, and the later moment when he will be killed. The silent square is a thin crescent, waiting for the rest of the circle to show up:

> The treacherous square held death.

The enemy soldiers are closer. Now we see them through Mathieu's eyes. Every detail stands out, because Mathieu is really looking at a choice. Is he going to fire on a soldier, or wait? The first shots ring out, from nearby. The future has begun. Mathieu looks round, and we suddenly get a different sense of time: 'Chasseriau … glanced at his wrist-watch … "Only three minutes since the motor cyclist went by."'

There is the steady drip-drip of the minutes, which contrasts with the intense feeling that a significant moment is at hand. The minutes are all equal, little empty 'nows', each alike. But through them all, from Mathieu's point of view, there runs a 'trajectory', which is his personal sense of the future.

His comrades are killed. The enemy is closing in. Surely this is the moment of necessity, when all control is lost? But for Sartre, freedom isn't about being 'in control' of events. It is about the experience of the world in terms of choice. For Mathieu, at last, the future is connected to his present acts. He pushes the trigger, and there is a consequence:

This *is* freedom, the experience of time as the unfolding of a possibility which would not exist if it were not for *his* presence in the world.

The climax is ambiguous, a death or an act, or just an idea finding its fulfilment at last:

> For years he had tried, in vain, to act ... But no one had stolen this! He had pressed a trigger and, for once, something had happened.

TIME AND COLLECTIVE PURPOSE

In Part II of *Iron in the Soul*, we enter the world of another modern condition, The Prison Camp. The main character now is Brunet, who appeared in *The Age of Reason* and *The Reprieve*, Mathieu's former friend who has become a functionary within the French Communist party. Brunet is one of the prisoners, but he experiences the world entirely from the point of view of his role as a revolutionary leader. For the revolutionary, everything in the present is potentially tied to a future of his own making. He scans the mob and sees them in terms of their potential for being re-made, almost as if they were material for art: 'Not easy material to work on.' They, on the other hand, have no sense of any future, because they have no feeling of being free agents. As they drift into the prison camp, time seems to be taken out of their hands altogether. For the inmates, time means 'routine', which is another kind of endless present tense. So we have two extreme versions of modern times:

> He was free.
> Fifteen minutes.

Character File: Brunet and The Crowd

Modern condition	Character	Experience of time	Date in history
The revolutionary	Brunet	Planning	Summer 1940
The inmate	Faceless	Routine	Summer 1940

Brunet then encounters Schneider, the replacement for Mathieu in this last part, a sceptic with a pragmatic commitment to his fellow men. Brunet asserts his plan, to 'sift out the healthy elements, organize them …' Schneider replies on behalf of a different vision:

> There's nothing we can do to influence the future one way or the other … if we can give them something to live for *here*.

Epilogue

Sartre intended to add a volume called *The Last Chance* to this sequence. Here Mathieu was apparently to revive and become a resistance leader along with Brunet. But Sartre finally surrendered his hold on that moment, as he told John Gerassi: 'I just couldn't make a situation which had been crucial and absolutely valid in 1942 relevant in 1950.' He remained faithful to time.

Sartre's Existentialism: Being Human, Being Unhappy

AN EXISTENTIAL VISION

At the heart of any account of Sartre is his 'Existentialism'. We have already seen several of the key elements: the approach to time and experience, freedom and the other. In this chapter, we will examine Existentialism as Sartre's philosophical *system*. However, within the system there is always a vision:

> Consciousness ... saw itself first of all as something completely gratuitous ... as something uncreated and unjustifiable whose only claim to existence was the mere fact that it already existed.
>
> From *Baudelaire* (1950)

Within this quote, there are the key definitions of Sartre's Existentialism. Existentialism is about the ways in which each human individual becomes conscious of their own *existence*.

Sartre's Existentialism: Key Definitions

- I am conscious of my existence without having any way of justifying or even explaining it.

- To become conscious means to recognize the gratuitousness of one's existence, that is, the lack of any reason linking your existence to any wider scheme of things.

- Your existence confronts you as a blank fact, without origin. You cannot find the meaning of your existence by asking where you come from.

The whole system develops in response to this central disturbing vision.

BEING AND NOTHINGNESS: THE SYSTEM

We have seen several times how Sartre presented ideas in *Being and Nothingness*. To understand the total system, we need to survey the work as a whole in outline. The book is designed to give expression to the central vision where a person becomes conscious of their own existence as 'gratuitous', 'unjustifiable', without origin or outside purpose. You can call this situation 'meaningless', or you can say that it is 'freedom', since nothing outside us sets our agenda.

The book is divided into four parts, each taking on a key idea.

Concept File: *Being and Nothingness* 1

Heading:	Nothingness.
Subject:	Our experience in terms of absence, loss, incompleteness.
Key quote:	'My freedom is anguished at being the foundation of values while itself without foundation.'

You could say that Sartre's philosophy is truly much ado about nothingness, a theme which he has taken over from Heidegger, whose influence we noted in the account of *Nausea*. When we become conscious of our own existence, we also become aware that it is founded upon 'nothing', since we have no support beneath us or before us. We exist, for ourselves, on the basis of 'nothing'. This feeling of being 'without foundation' is another way of talking about nothingness. But you can also see this nothingness as freedom. No outside authority dictates to any individual the meaning of their life. We are gratuitous, no outside plan has given a space to fit us. That also means each person is responsible for the meaning of their own life.

Concept File: *Being and Nothingness* II

Heading:	Being-For-Itself.
Subject:	Human 'consciousness' and its 'reflectiveness', its awareness of itself.
Key quote:	'One suffers and one suffers from not suffering enough.'

In Part II, Sartre moves on to consider 'the being of the self'. As we have noted above, the central term is 'consciousness', and Sartre is particularly interested in how we become conscious of ourselves or, you could say, how our consciousness is aware of itself. His term for this self-awareness is 'reflectiveness', as if we have an inner mirror in which consciousness sees itself.

For Sartre, there is something terrifying about our reflectiveness. It means that I can never be truly spontaneous, never even completely myself. I am always aware of myself, and so there is always something outside the experience, however intense or sincere or important it may be. I may be suffering terribly, mourning the greatest loss. But, for

Sartre, there will always be something removed, outside the feeling, looking on. I will always feel that I could be doing more justice to the loss, I could be more authentic than I am.

Concept File: *Being and Nothingness* III

Heading:	Being-For-Others.
Subject:	The shaping of each person from within by the presence of 'the Other'.
Key quote:	'Consciousness is affirmed in the face of the Other.'

So far Sartre has been examining the truth of the individual, who is ultimately alone in the universe and responsible for his or her own life. But in Part III we find the other side of the truth being emphasized, the truth that no one can be conscious of their own life except in relation to 'the Other'. We do not form our identity first, and then turn outward to look at others. On the contrary, the look which the Other turns on us is there inside all our attempts to create an identity. I have to make my own self, true, but all my efforts are always directed towards my sense of this Other. How I think I am regarded shapes everything I do to make my own life.

Concept File: *Being and Nothingness* IV

Heading:	Having, Being and Doing.
Subject:	Freedom and 'the given' facts.
Key quote:	'I prepare the ground for the revelation of my environment.'

The world, my 'environment', seems to rise up and confront me as a fact, or a wall of 'given' situations, in Sartre's terms. But in Part IV, he insists that I am the one who is responsible for the way this world appears before me. The facts are there, they are real: but I am still responsible for their *meaning*, and so I am still the one who has chosen this world, and who will choose its futures. This is not a bland notion of 'freedom'. Indeed Sartre sees this freedom as 'adversity', as struggle: but being free remains 'the primitive structure of the situation', the burden we cannot escape.

THE EXISTENTIAL CONDITION

Let us now close in on the Existential vision of the human condition which is most urgently expressed by Part II of *Being and Nothingness*. Three principles can be defined:

1 Being Human Means Being Unhappy

The central problem is what it means to be human. Sartre has many answers to this single question, but one of the most striking is that being human means being unhappy. The vision is quite explicit:

> Human reality therefore is by nature an unhappy consciousness with no possibility of surpassing its unhappy state.

I have not a single moment's respite until I die: the world will never come to me pure and simple, and nor will my own feelings or perceptions. I always have this burden of being conscious. This is the unhappy state which I can never reach beyond, and it is why Sartre uses metaphors like haunting to describe the existential condition of humanity, the nature of our existence.

2 Each Human Consciousness Exists 'for-itself'

In Sartre's existential theory, the world can be divided into two camps. First, there is the 'in itself'. By this term, Sartre means all those things which just are what they are. For example, a table is just a table, neither more nor less. But being human is not like that. We belong to what is termed 'being-for-itself'. This is a major distinction in Sartre's thought.

The crucial feature of being human is that we constantly appear before our own consciousness. We are never just here in the world. We are also aware of ourselves. In us, being exists 'for itself'; in tables, being is simply there.

In a stunning phrase, the language of an artist or a poet, Sartre declares that human consciousness is 'a decompression of being'. The table is tightly packed together: everything about it is sitting there. But something in us is different. There is some kind of space separating us from ourselves, whereas nothing stands between a table and itself. Here lies another clue to the unhappiness of being human. We are only able to be baffled by ourselves because we are never completely inside our life. We are always the audience as well as the actor.

3 There is Always a Witness

It would be fairly commonplace to say that people never just act, they are always aware of acting. I can't just open a door; I also notice myself opening it. For Sartre, the real problem is our thoughts themselves, and also our feelings. He gives the example of belief: a belief is never just a belief, like an object is an object. Sartre argues that you can never say 'that my belief is my belief'. We can't ever have a simple experience of believing. We are always also witnesses to our beliefs. Now, for Sartre, this is a terrible fact about human beings. He calls this 'existing for a witness' and declares it to be 'nullifying'. We are never just ourselves, not even in our inmost thought and feelings:

> Neither belief nor pleasure nor joy can exist before being conscious, consciousness is the measure of their being.

Of course, people sometimes feel happy. Sartre is not arguing that happiness is an illusion, like some religious thinkers. But happiness is always troubled, just as belief is: we cannot just *be* happy. We also notice, and therefore question, our own feeling. Sartre himself calls the impact of this awareness 'shattering'.

To sum up: you can live your whole life in the hope of one day being yourself, and feeling, as they say, at home in your skin. But, in this existential story, that moment of 'one-ness' will never arrive. I feel sad and, at the same moment, I am aware of myself being sad. Immediately, I can ask whether the feeling is genuine, justified or just a bit of a drama. I can't ever feel sad, not even at the most heart-rending moment, without this gap appearing, across which I can wonder about myself.

Being and Nothingness is a vast system of ideas; but at its heart are certain experiences. The book is an attempt to put into words the common things in our lives which defy expression. Sartre believes we have hidden these difficult questions behind facile answers. His aim is to confront us with the insoluble riddle of our own being.

Eternity, 1944:
'Hell is Other People'

7

EXISTENTIAL HELL

In this chapter, we shall look at how the theory of 'unhappy consciousness' is given body in other works by Sartre from during and just after the Second World War. These are Sartre's visions of hell and, over the gateway hangs the most famous sentence from any of his works, a sentence spoken by the character called Garcin in his play *In Camera* (or *No Exit*):

Hell is ... other people.

Our subject is now Existentialism as the theory of hell. In the context of the Second World War, one can see how such a theory fulfilled a deep need in western thought.

The crucial idea is that each of us is burdened by an endless consciousness, which constantly reflects back on itself – each exists in the realm of this 'for itself'. Yet each of us seeks relief from this eternal 'reflectiveness' – relief which can only be found in the eyes of another. Hence the self is, as Sartre says in *Being and Nothingness*, 'affirmed in the face of the Other'. Only from the perspective of others, can we ever hope to experience the self as if it were fixed, stable, here and now. Otherwise, we have to live with the awful 'decompression of being', the sense of never being quite here, never being just like this.

We will now look at two Sartrean hells, both dating from the later years of the Second World War and attaining their controversial impact in the immediate post-war period. First, there is the play *In Camera*, which is literally set in hell. Then there is probably Sartre's most controversial text, *Anti-Semite and Jew*, which was conceived right at the end of the war, published in an early form in 1945 and finalized in

1948. Together, these texts illuminate one of the darkest moments in human history, and reflect upon dateless questions of suffering and evil.

IN CAMERA: HELL, 1944

Sartre's play *In Camera* was produced towards the end of the Nazi occupation of Paris in 1944, and belongs to the period of gathering resistance. Though permitted by the authorities, it was clearly understood at the time as a work of protest, at the very least a demand for action and commitment. Yet it was also, and remains, a profound realization of the condition of captivity and despair, of what such a condition would be like if allowed to continue indefinitely, if there was no hope of change.

Three individuals are conducted by a valet into a rather grand old-fashioned drawing-room, in hell. They do not know each other. Each has recently died, and there is no ambiguity about their situation: this is their hell, and they are here because of things they have done, or been, on earth. Each can glimpse the other world, though with fading clarity.

Throughout, they ask themselves, and each other, two questions: What have we done wrong to put ourselves here? and Why are we together? They soon realize that their purpose must be to inflict on one another the modern equivalent of the medieval tortures of the traditional underworld.

The three individuals, it turns out, have made their lives from the suffering they inflicted on others. The first, Garcin, has been executed by the army, apparently a noble end for a pacifist hero.

Character File: Joseph Garcin

Coward	Editor of a pacifist paper, has fled to the border on being called up.
Hypocrite	Has presented himself as generous, rescuing his wife 'from the gutter', but has, in fact, tortured her.

| Unfaithful | Has betrayed his wife with others. |
| Vain | Concerned only to *appear* admirable. |

This was a life compounded of pretences and a death undergone in terror.

The second individual, Inez, the poor postal clerk, seems at least clear-headed compared to the vain and over-blown Garcin. But she turns out to be as lethally dependent on others as he, and in as destructive a way.

Character File: Inez Serrano

Treacherous	Has taken over the life of another woman, Florence, wife of her cousin, while staying with the couple.
Cruel	After the two have left together, and the man has been killed in an accident, she tortures Florence with daily reminders of his death.
Heartless	Sees others only as vehicles for her own use, to relieve herself of her own emptiness.
Lethal	Florence has gassed both herself and Inez in the night, taking to three the number of the dead.

Inez has needed the suffering of others to affirm her own being. If Garcin has made his life of vanity, then she is cruelty.

The third character and apparently the mildest of the three, Estelle, turns out to be the active killer. Each of the others has caused death, but Estelle has committed the deed:

Character File: Estelle Rigault

Avaricious	Married an older man for money without love or kindness.
Lustful	Pursued younger men.
Vain	Has lived to be admired by men.
False	Betrayed not only her husband but her lovers.
Murderous	Has thrown her baby from balcony into lake below.

These are people in flight from their own nothingness and are infinitely destructive in the process.

The three make a perfect trinity of torturers. Each is in flight from their own consciousness, seeking the solidity that one only has in the eyes of another person. And each then is perfectly adapted to denying that relief to the others. The harder Garcin seeks reassurance that he is justified, the less the others will grant it to him. Estelle offers her body, but angrily dismisses his appeal for trust. Inez endlessly mocks all his efforts to present a plausible self. But then again Inez *needs* to be taken seriously as a person who matters enough to be the supreme torturer of Estelle for whom she can never have any real significance, being 'merely' a woman. Estelle turns to the eyes of the others, and finds none of the need which she in turns needs:

> *Inez* Hullo, what's that – that nasty red spot at the bottom of your cheek? A pimple?
> *Estelle* A pimple? Oh, how simply foul. Where?
> *Inez* There ... There isn't any pimple, not a trace of one. So what about it? Suppose the mirror started telling lies.

In this mirrorless room, there is no refuge from the eyes of the Other, for someone who has no courage to face their own consciousness, to take responsibility for who they are or what they have become. These are people for whom that responsibility is unbearable. Therefore, they are flung on the resources of the other and tortured without mercy. If Estelle were able to make the authentic choice to be herself, then she could overcome Inez's mirror torture – but she is infinitely dependent on the affirming gaze of the Other. On the other hand, Inez can never really be happy, because her power is too limited. Estelle does not really depend upon her at all:

> *Estelle* But I wish he'd notice me, too.
> *Inez* Of course! Because he's a Man!

But when Garcin wants to exploit that hold, that need, he too in turn is disappointed. he asks, 'Well, Estelle, am I a coward?' And Estelle replies, 'How can I say?'

His turn to Inez completes the circle of hell:

> *Garcin* So it's you whom I have to convince; you are of my kind. ... If you'll have faith in me I'm saved.

He receives from Inez the deadly reply, 'Now then! Don't lose heart. It shouldn't be too hard, convincing me.'

Endlessly, they will turn to one another, to find themselves thrown back upon their own emptiness. These are people who cannot live with their own freedom. They have chosen this suffering in preference to the only alternative, the authentic choice, the responsible choice of a life from one's own unsupported perspective. No wonder, for them, as Garcin says at the end:

> Hell is ... other people!

ANTI-SEMITE AND JEW: HISTORY AS HELL

This work, first written in 1945 and given final form in 1948, was among Sartre's most controversial. It starts from the situation after the war and the holocaust:

> Today those Jews whom the Germans did not deport or murder are coming back to their homes.

Sartre was protesting against the beginning of a great silence:

> Do we say anything about the Jews? Do we give a though to those who died in the gas chambers at Lublin?

This too is an attempt to understand the making of a modern hell, with all its physical and mental tortures. The book presents a number of 'characters': the anti-Semite, the democrat and, in different forms, the Jew. It is the presentation of the Jewish figures that has made the book controversial, even scandalous.

This hell is seen to arise from the interplay of these figures and, most importantly, from the nature of the anti-Semite. Sartre sees anti-Semitism as a major trait of the western world, including the French world. He characterizes the anti-Semite as someone 'attracted by the durability of a stone'. For the anti-Semite, human freedom is unbearable: 'It is as if their own existence were in continual suspension.' In other words, these are people like the characters in *In Camera*, for whom their own consciousness is an intolerable weight. Like Garcin and Estelle and Inez, 'they wish to exist all at once and right away'. They cannot possibly create such a being from within and, therefore, they demand that others give them this solidity that they find lacking. Anti-Semitism is the flight from unhappy consciousness. This works in a number of ways. First, the anti-Semite plunges into a mass of other anti-Semites, and so loses the sense of individual responsibility. Then the contrast with the supposed Jew provides an apparently stable frame of reference within which to live out this falsely secure being. For the anti-Semite, the Jew is a fixed 'essence' of evil and, in the face of that 'Other', the anti-Semite lives secure in his own being, outside the human condition of responsibility.

The democrat figures briefly as a false alternative, the weak liberal who comes to the defence of the Jew only on the basis of a dilute theory of universal human nature. For Sartre, that too is a flight from existence. There is, in existential terms, no such human nature to save any of us from our individual plight. To say that the Jew is human 'like us', is to offer an empty defence: no one can say what being human means. Then comes the attempt to represent the Jewish figure. Here Sartre makes his most controversial move:

> The Jew is one whom other men consider a Jew ...

He denies to Judaism any inner principle or meaning. For Sartre, Jewishness is a condition defined entirely by the hostile Other, by the anti-Semitic world. The Jew, in Sartre's terms, is a function of the anti-Semitic need for such a figure:

> Thus the Jew is in the situation of a Jew because he lives in the midst of
> a society that takes him for a Jew.

This statement, made in the aftermath of the holocaust, and at the time of the founding of Israel, was capable of being seen itself as a philosophical form of the anti-Semitism Sartre was so passionately condemning. It seems Sartre himself could not stand outside the hell of otherness which he was envisioning.

Sartre then tries to distinguish between authentic and inauthentic ways of being a Jew. The inauthentic version mode involves denial of the situation – the authentic starts from within it:

> Authenticity ... consists in having a true and lucid consciousness of
> the situation.

Sartre makes clear that he thinks there are far more inauthentic Christians than Jews, but he has in effect taken an approach which could explain why it is so hard for a Jew to be authentic.

Sartre's hells belong to their time, and to no specific time. They express the concepts of human consciousness defended by *Being and Nothingness*, the burden of endless 'reflectiveness' combined with the infinite dependence on 'the Other'. But there is also a streak of compassion in these texts which leads towards the next phase under consideration, Sartre and liberation.

24 August 1944, Paris: Liberation of Humanity

8

THE THINKER AS SYMBOL

Sartre has become one of the symbols of the twentieth century. He represents a certain idea of 'the intellectual', a symbolism which echoes far beyond his specific philosophies. Now we come to the central moment in the creation of the symbolic Sartre: the liberation of the city of Paris from the Nazis in August 1944. Sartre has come down to us as one of the symbols of the liberation of Paris, of France and of Europe. At the start of the twenty-first century, Jean-Paul Sartre remains an icon of the twentieth century, the thinker of the liberation.

The day of this liberation was 24 August 1944, when the fighters of the French Resistance witnessed the flight of their Nazi occupiers from Paris. This was a politically complex moment. There had been days of fierce fighting inside the city, and the Allied armies were advancing on the capital. From the French point of view, it was vital that they should be seen to have liberated themselves, their own capital, before their liberators arrived. Sartre was in Paris at this time and his writings have contributed to the collective memory of those days. At the time, he wrote a kind of journal of the liberation for Camus's resistance paper *Le Combat*. But the most important version of this day itself was written exactly one year later, on 24 August 1945, as the first commemoration took place. One might say that Sartre's article entitled 'The Liberation of Paris' helped to forge the post-war idea of liberation, and belongs to the immediate creation of the post-war era. Here Sartre's writing was directly *about* a date, 24 August; but being Sartre, he sought to give that date a universal significance, not just for that nation or even for that generation, but for humanity. In this post-war moment, Sartre re-made himself as a philosopher of humanity, and Existentialism as a philosophy of human liberation.

KEY MOMENT: 24 AUGUST 1944 – DATE OF LIBERATION

Looking at the first anniversary of the liberation, in the journal *Clarté*, Sartre asked a strange-sounding question: 'What is being celebrated in this way?' He then refuses to give the obvious answer, French freedom, the defeat of the Nazis. There is something deeper, more lasting behind this date, something more has been liberated:

> I realise that it is mankind and his powers.

Here Sartre is announcing a central concept in the next phase of his thinking – the concept of 'humanity'. This is, of course, an old idea, which had been important to French politics since the Revolution of 1789. But what was Sartre doing talking of this humanity? What did he have to do with an idea of shared and even universal interconnection? On the face of it, 'humanity' was exactly the kind of notion which Sartre had been dedicated to erasing in his assault on traditional consolations and values. Had he returned to the fold of western tradition, accepted the old ideas after all? Was Sartre, in the end, going to speak on behalf of exactly the kind of consoling abstractions which *Being and Nothingness* had been devoted to eliminating from the philosophical language of the future?

As we shall see, Sartre was trying to use this great term, 'humanity', in his own way, to pass it on to the post-war era in a modern form.

Concept File: Humanity

- This Humanity is a continuous *creation*. Each of us makes and re-makes constantly the idea of humanity.

- Humanity doesn't mean 'human nature', which would have contradicted the basic principles of Sartre's existentialism. *There is no fixed 'human essence'.*

- This humanity is an ethical idea: you should choose and judge your *acts* in relation to *humanity as a whole*.

This notion of humanity was, as we shall see, Sartre's major contribution to the immediate post-war moment. The essay on the liberation of Paris makes 24 August 1944 into a key date when humanity entered into a new moment, a time of new creation. This moment applied not just to Parisians or the Resistance or French people. Looking at this date of 24 August in retrospect, the question arises: Is this declaration anything more than sentimentalism? Has Sartre given in to conventional notions after all his efforts at starting again?

There are several points which can be made in defence of Sartre's post-war 'humanity':

First, for Sartre, it is the concrete experience of the war which has created this new humanity:

> The liberation of Paris, an episode in a war that covered the whole world, was a joint action on the part of all the Allied armies.

This means that Sartre's humanity is not a mysterious abstraction. He is, in many ways, anticipating current day thinking about *globalization*, the ending of the era when nations or regions or cities were autonomous.

Second, this humanity is not a reassuring constant. On the contrary, humanity is a name for what is at stake at this moment of global crisis, when the American atom bombs have just fallen on Hiroshima and Nagasaki to bring about the final surrender of Japan:

> …that the anniversary of the Parisian uprising should fall so close to the first appearance of the atomic bomb.

For Sartre, 1945 was adding a new meaning to 24 August. This bomb is 'the negation of mankind'. So Sartre is talking about a human *idea* which is being contested by contrasting human choices and acts. On the one hand, there are acts which re-create the ideal of the human, like the liberation of Paris. On the other hand, there is the threat of ultimate destruction.

Third, the term 'humanity' is a way of talking about how freedom entered the world. The resistance fighters enacted human freedom on behalf of all people:

> But what these men intended was precisely to reject destiny.

To act in the name of humanity means to reassert your own individual responsibility. If you act in the name of humanity, you will constantly face up to the question: What should I do now? You will have no excuses, no ideas of necessity to let you off the hook.

But there are also things to be said against Sartre's association of the idea of humanity with 24 August 1944.

First, there is a current of nationalism running through the argument about the liberation of humanity. In Sartre's vision, the French resistance are asserting human potential not only against Nazism, but also against the new American-dominated order to come, which is seen as 'rather inhuman'. Might there not be a lingering prejudice at work in such comments?

Second, though you could say it was understandable, at times the idea of Paris itself seems sentimental:

> The whole history of Paris was there, in that sun …

Contemplating this date, Sartre had clearly felt impelled to make an affirmation, and so he called upon humanity. The result was one of the major moments in the public influence of philosophy.

'EXISTENTIALISM AND HUMANISM'

On the evening of 28 October 1945, Sartre gave one of the most important public addresses by a philosopher in modern times. Facing a packed audience, in the immediate aftermath of the war, he delivered a speech in defence of Existentialism as a 'doctrine' for the age, indeed the only possible doctrine with which people could confront the prospect of rebuilding their world. This Parisian speech takes forward the essential concept of humanity we have seen, in view of the liberation of that city.

This lecture was revised and later published as 'The Humanism of Existentialism' or *Existentialism and Humanism*, but its influence was already immense. Sartre had brought Paris to the centre of the post-war world, as the capital of the new vision. Even as the rigidity of the Cold War was replacing the struggle with Fascism, Sartre stood for a new path, a different way.

Sartre gave his tightest definition of Existentialism, as the philosophy for which:

> existence precedes essence.

What he meant was that, in the case of human beings, we find ourselves cast into the world before we have any way to define who we are or why we exist. He contrasts this condition with that of a tool which we make in order to perform a certain purpose, and which therefore has an essence waiting for it before it ever exists. While he recognizes that there are Christian Existentialists, Sartre insists that his 'atheistic' approach is most consistent with the true existential principle, since Christians can always say that God created man with an idea in view.

Sartre is now insisting that Existentialism is a doctrine, where previously it seemed more like an approach or a way of asking questions of our experience. Given the context of liberation and loss, you can see why Sartre felt the need to offer more of a positive answer both to his immediate listeners and to the post-war world. As with the article, the answer hinges on Sartre's idea of humanity, now taken further and made into a kind of Humanist Manifesto.

Sartre gives us certain basic definitions with which to orient our thinking, and our decisions.

Concept file: Existential Humanism

Key definition: MAN

- 'Man' is that being for whom 'existence precedes essence'. There is no human soul or essence prior to our choices.

- 'Man' is first of all 'nothing'. He has no given nature.

On the face of it, this doesn't sound much like humanism, the faith in humanity. But this approach is brilliantly adapted to a world which has been reduced to rubble in so many of its main centres. This is a definition of 'man' for an age of reconstruction.

Though Sartre continues to reject human nature, he restores the idea of shared humanity by talking about a human condition, a fundamental situation that is common to all.

Concept File: Existential Humanism

Key definition: HUMAN CONDITION

- The human condition is one of 'forlornness': ' God does not exist and that we have to face all the consequences of this.'

To say that our condition is 'forlorn' seems depressing, but Sartre intends the idea to have a positive potential. No higher power fixes our lives for us. Left alone in the world, each of us is free to decide his or her own fate, to reconstruct our being from inside.

Sartre is giving universal meaning to many people's experience of *being* at the end of the war. Others will re-make humanity in the future, and that will decide the meaning of this past, which is, at the same time, a completed thing.

Concept file: Existential Humanism

> Key definition: THE FUTURE/TOMORROW
>
> • The future is the empty space that makes us free. Since 'men are free', it is 'tomorrow' that they will 'freely decide what man will be.'

Many have died, many have acted, others have suffered. No one can say what these happenings mean yet, because humanity itself is yet to be decided. The Nazis have just been defeated. But Sartre insists that, like every other possibility, Fascism remains a potential future:

Tomorrow after my death, some men may decide to set up Fascism, and the others may be cowardly and muddled enough to let them do it. Fascism will then be the human reality ...

Man is 'nothing', until he remakes his own image. The human condition is forlorn, and no outside agency will rescue us from our own ideas or actions. The future is always empty, a free space to be recreated by others. No one can say, finally, what 24 August 1944 means. It had a meaning then, and another on its first anniversary, in the light of Hiroshima. If 20 years later, Fascism returns in triumph, 24 August will, like the human condition of which it is part, take yet another turn.

Post-War, City Streets: Modern Being

THE POST-WAR SARTRE

After the war, Sartre pursued the Existential question: What is the meaning of our human being? But increasingly, he moved beyond his previous Existential answer. The key to this development was his concern with society. To some extent, he became more political and, as we shall see, Marxism moves to the centre of his thought. But he did not turn away from his previous concerns; rather, he saw them in a changing perspective.

This was the period of the Cold War, the dangerous balance of hostility between a capitalist West and an East dominated by Stalin's USSR. This conflict was kept from breaking into a third world war, and Europe avoided large-scale military action. However, elsewhere the battle was fought out – in the Korean war and later in Vietnam, as well as many other conflicts. Over the whole scene, there was the shadow of the atom bomb, being developed on both sides, and already used by the US against Japan at the end of the Second World War.

One of the ways in which Sartre tried to understand this changing world was by thinking about the world's great cities and about urban life. In this topical writing, Sartre remained faithful to the ideal of the writer, or the prose writer, which he expressed in *What is Literature?* (or 'What is Writing?'), his post-war literary manifesto that first appeared in *Modern Times* in 1947. The true writer 'has chosen to reveal the world', so that humanity may 'assume full responsibility before the object which has been thus laid bare'. This is the work of the committed writer: not preaching or moralizing, but the free disclosure of the world so that others may achieve their freedom in the face of this revelation.

SARTRE'S CITIES

After the war, Sartre became a great traveller, as well as increasingly a symbol of his own city, Paris. He visited many of the great cities where the idea of the modern world was being re-shaped, often at historically significant moments in their stories.

Sartre File: Post-War Cities

Place	Time	Key Quote
Paris	1944	'…the whole history of Paris was there, in that sun.'
New York	1945	'…space crosses through New York, the great empty space of the steppes or the pampas.'
Rome	1952	'…thirty centuries have impregnated its walls with phosphorus.'
Venice	1953	'…searching for the secret Venice on the far side …Venice is wherever I am not.'
Havana	1960	'A great flood of electric light … the endless parade of cars.'

Sartre was not an ordinary travel writer. He wrote about particular places, at specific moments, but he was always asking general questions. This is consistent with Sartre's philosophy: he found no way to approach universal problems except through specific objects, people, places and actions.

In his essay on New York, Sartre wrote that all Europeans 'subsist on the myth of the great city which we created in the nineteenth century.' In other words, cities are also *myths*: they embody the shared pool of ideas which people use to give meaning to their individual lives. Being Jean-Paul means being a European, which is all about the ideal of an ancient urban civilization. If you sit outside a Paris café, as a French person, as a European, you are realizing your own being within that shared myth. The weight of the old city 'weighs heavily on the earth', and you feel your own being sharing in that solid presence.

By contrast, Sartre interpreted New York in terms of a different urban myth, the city of space, the open city. This place, in 1946, represents a wide horizon, the vista of the unexplored, the pioneer ideal. As a European, Sartre experiences this myth from outside, and realizes his own alien being by contrast. Here is the map of Sartre's urban myths, cities that stand for different modes of modern being.

Concept File: Urban Myths

Paris, 1944	City of Liberation
New York, 1945	City of Emptiness
Rome, 1952	City of Survivals
Venice, 1953	City of Absence
Havana, 1960	City on Parade

Each of these cities is there in modern consciousness, and when we visit them we have the strange experience of facing outside ourselves ideas that are already inside us. Sartre is, among other things, the great philosopher of urban tourism.

In many ways, Sartre's cities form a system of contrasts. If New York stands for space, almost for the empty city, then Rome is the city of closure, the walled city. These aren't only contrasts of landscape: they stand, according to Sartre, for different ways of being, both individually and socially. In Rome, the past lives on as the smell of the

walls. Phosphorus is a violent element, the very opposite of stable and solid: these walls have stood there forever, yet they smell of violence and mutability. Although New York's prairies are open, they also seem to dwarf all human actions; there is no way anyone could leave a mark on these empty vistas. In Rome, you feel that every wall is about to vaporize, so intense is the feeling of demonic energy left by history: yet nothing does change. In New York, you feel that everything is open, possibilities are limitless, and yet none of them counts for anything in the end. These cities stand for different failures to live with the real facts of human freedom.

Venice and Havana offer a different contrast. Venice is always falling away, slipping just out of reach: this city is like the modern self, whose nature it is to slip endlessly away: the harder you look, the further off it seems. But Havana rushes out to meet your gaze: it is a city on display and of display. There are no secrets on those streets, where instead an unending 'parade' marches past. Yet when you look closer, you see that the parade is composed of old American cars, it doesn't belong here at all, and so the scene also seems to point elsewhere, to slip away.

Sartre's post-war cities are maps of hope and disappointment. In each case, he sees an appeal, an idea which seems worthwhile. There are vivid instants and images, when the city seems to come into its own. Yet each time, there seems to be a basic flaw, something illusory or treacherous. These cities are places where hope has been tried and found wanting.

KEY MOMENT: BUS QUEUE, RUE SAINT-GERMAIN, 1950s

Sartre felt there is another side to the meaning of the modern city in our lives. Cities are the scene of most of our everyday lives, and in a way the city *stands for* the routine world, the conventional pattern of modern living. In the 1950s, Sartre made a detailed interpretation of one of the most banal of all scenes in modern urban life. The passage forms a long section of a book written from 1957 and finally published in 1960, entitled forbiddingly *The Critique of Dialectical Reason*. We will be looking later at that work more generally, but for the moment let us close in on Sartre's bus queue, and modern being.

Sartre sets the scene. There is a group of people in Paris, in a central square called the Place Saint-Germain: 'They are waiting for a bus at a bus stop in front of the church.' This is a particular place and time. Sartre is interested in how these people are, and aren't, related to each other as they stand in the queue. Each person is standing on their own, yet they are also being an ensemble. In a leap of perspective, Sartre labels the queue:

a plurality of isolations.

Queuing for this bus is a way of being alone. Sartre assumes no one is with a child, a friend, a lover, because this is a commuter bus on the way to work in the morning. That in itself tells you a lot about the nature of the post-war world he is interpreting: work is one life, home another. But there is a paradox about the bus queue version of being alone. You need to be with other people in order to be isolated in this way. From *Nausea* onwards, Sartre has been pursuing this question of isolation.

Now he talks of 'the isolation which everyone lives', standing on that pavement, in that city, in that modern world. Isolation is a way of being in the world.

The bus queue *is* the city as a way of life, beyond the monuments and the grand histories. If you want a representative character for the 1950s, you might well choose the urban commuter, whose basic characteristics emerge in the queue:

Character File: The Urban Commuter

Quality	Key Quote
Deliberate **Isolation**.	'... he turns his back upon his neighbour.'
Conformity without connection.	'...the mode of life occasions isolated behaviour in everyone – buying the paper as you leave the house, reading it on the bus.'

Compliance instead of dialogue.	'the travellers waiting for the bus take tickets indicating their order of arrival.'
Unity without community.	'the unity of the commuters lies in the bus they are waiting for.'

This urban commuter is an absolutely integrated character, whose life is shaped by a kind of belonging so intense that it leaves little space for individual expression. This character wants to be part of a city, a society, a world – but what a way to belong!

The queue is also a way of solving a practical problem which lies behind all social and especially all *economic* systems:

There are not enough places for everyone.

Societies come into existence as answers to this problem. But the urban commuter is denied access to most of the richer ways of approaching such problems, such as dialogue or communal choice or even heroic contest. There is a system at work and it replaces contact and community as the answer to this problem of 'too few places'. Sartre's term for this condition is 'seriality', or life as a series, a line or a list or a sequence. In a series, one element simply comes after the other, without any distinction or choice. The series is an absolutely reduced way of being together, without ever forming a conscious or communicative group. The urban commuter of the 1950s is a character fitted to living life in series, and banal urban life is the perfect expression of this seriality.

Sartre's Second Existentialism: A Radical Philosophy

THE LATER PHILOSOPHY

As a thinker, Sartre is most famous for the system expressed by *Being and Nothingness*, and expanded in the fiction and drama of the 1930s and 1940s. But as we have already seen, he was far from finished after the war. Through the fifties, Sartre the man was involved in the world of public controversies, and his fame as a thinker and writer became a weapon to be exploited in these conflicts. The man who had theorized about the individual was increasingly a participant in group protests, even a spokesman for mass movements. In 1954, for example, he became vice-president of the France–USSR Association, a role in which he campaigned against the increasingly 'hot' Cold War between the West and the Soviet bloc. In 1956, the Russian forces invaded Hungary, to crush a more liberal regime that had emerged in their satellite state. Sartre resigned from his role in the Association and wrote in defence of the Hungarians. By 1960, Sartre was in Cuba, meeting Fidel Castro and Che Guevara, both in their different ways icons of the protests movements to emerge in the 1960s. At the same time he re-made his philosophy in *The Critique of Dialectical Reason*, published in 1960.

The Critique of Dialectical Reason: What Does the Title Mean?

Critique

Whenever any philosopher calls their book, 'Critique', they are pointing back to the monumental works of the German Romantic thinker, Immanuel Kant, especially his *Critique of Pure Reason*, *Critique of Practical Reason* and *Critique of Judgement*. So part of the meaning is: here is a major work, since Kant's books are often accepted as the founding works of modern philosophy. In this context, 'critique' doesn't mean 'tearing apart' or 'writing against'. On the contrary, this kind of critique is meant to be an analysis of something designed to put it on a firmer footing than has so far been possible. So Kant's critique of pure reason was designed to criticize the previous defences of reason, and to offer new principles. Sartre's 'critique' is designed to provide a new basis for whatever is meant by 'dialectical reason', not to dispose of it.

Dialectical

Originally, 'dialectic' was an ancient Greek term for the true philosophical method, as presented in the Dialogues of Plato. The basis of this method was the use of contradiction and conflict to test and develop ideas. Plato argued that the true method must employ antithesis, the collision of contrasting proposals and visions, which would then come together to create a new and higher truth. However, the term 'dialectic' was, by 1960, firmly associated with the philosophy of Marxism, where it had been used since the nineteenth century to describe the fundamental movement of human history and even of the natural world. In the Marxist version, history was seen as a process driven forwards by a dialectical collision of opposing forces. The main examples, in modern times, of such opposing forces were the two great social classes of industrial society: the working-class and the bourgeoisie, or the owners. Slightly confusingly, Marxism also used the term 'dialectical' to describe its own methods of analysis, and referred to its main doctrines as 'dialectical materialism'. This meant essentially that the great conflicts had a material or economic basis. It wasn't abstract ideas that were in opposition, but real groups of people driven on by concrete needs and desires.

Reason

Kant had originally written his critiques about different forms of human reason. Sartre was, in his title, returning to this grand philosophical task: he wanted to rewrite the basic definitions of what it means to think and act rationally, what counts as a reasoned understanding of the world, as against mere prejudice or fantasy or emotion. Dialectical reason means the kind of thinking which uses oppositions and conflicts to work out its ideas about the world, and so here Sartre was looking back to the ancient Greeks. The main alternative by 1960, however, was what Sartre called 'scientific reason', which works by experiment and proof. Sartre did not deny science, but he wanted dialectical reason to be its equal. Above all, he believed that dialectic was a superior approach to science for the understanding of society and history.

The Critique of Dialectical Reason

> In the end, this means that we are confronted again with the need to establish the dialectic as the universal method and universal law of anthropology.

In a nutshell, Sartre wanted to show that there was a better way to be rational about human history than anyone had yet worked out. This is clearly a massive ambition. True, the whole project feels drier and less immediate than the Existentialism of *Being and Nothingness* and *The Roads to Freedom*. But in many ways Sartre remains faithful to the basic vision of that first wave. His claim had been that the Existentialist could give a true picture of individual experience and the human condition approached through that experience. His later claim is that Existentialism had the power to rescue Marxism and world philosophy generally from false assumptions about society and history.

Here 'anthropology' means the social study of humanity. The language may sound technical, even a touch turgid, compared to the literary excitement of the earlier philosophy, but the scale is still inspiring. Sartre argues that the world has lost touch with the basic methods for understanding human society and development. We have no approach which is specifically designed for understanding ourselves, however successful we have been in understanding nature.

'MAN' AND 'NATURE': THE NEW DIALECTIC

Sartre's earlier work had been based on a vision of the human condition, seen primarily in terms of the absolute and terrible freedom of the individual, burdened with a consciousness which could never justify itself. His later work also starts from a definition of the human lot, but in collective terms:

> Thus, the history of man is an adventure of nature.

This is a good example of 'dialectic' in operation. There are two opposing terms inside this proposition: 'man' and 'nature'. Sartre brings the two together and from the collision he creates a third term: 'history'. This is a pretty radical revision of the normal sense of 'history', which usually means the human story as performed by heroes and villains, wars and inventions. For Sartre, history is simultaneously human action and the 'adventure' of something that is not specifically human at all, which he calls nature.

Here the later dialectical Sartre turns out to be very much in tune with the earlier Existential-thinking Sartre. History belongs to 'man', except that there is really no such thing as this 'man'. As an Existentialist, Sartre began by rejecting all fixed definitions of what it means to be human. There is no human essence. To be human is whatever we make of it. Now he is applying that same Existential approach to history as a whole. History cannot be the story of humanity, in any stable sense, since humanity is precisely what changes as a result. History is the story of a *quest* whose goal may be humanity, but which has never reached any such end-point.

Here is the basic layout of the human condition in these dialectical terms:

Concept File: The Human Dialectic

Man is …	Key Quote	Comment
A Material Being.	'man is a material organism.'	The search for humanity is not spiritual. It is about real needs and survival.
A Product.	'worked matter produces man.'	We are what the world around allows us to make of ourselves.
A Producer.	'produces or uses this worked matter.'	But the world is also what we make and how we make it.

RED–GREEN SARTRE

As we shall see in the next chapter, Sartre was trying to create a new basis for Marxist politics, to set against the Soviet-dominated models of the 1950s. But before we look more closely at this 'Red Sartre', it is worth pausing over the principles behind his arguments – principles which begin with this connection between man and nature. Sartre was developing an ecological approach which reaches beyond the political issues of his time, and continues to talk to our current concerns.

The examples discussed in the *Critique* are of two kinds. There are extensive discussions of political and social revolution using, on the whole, instances from the French Revolution of 1789. But there are at least as many passages dealing with what we would now call environmental crises and problems.

Concept file: Sartre's Dialectical Ecology

Crisis	Example	Key concept
Flooding	Chinese peasant land.	'negation.'
Pollution	Nineteenth-century city air.	'counter finality.'

Take first the problem of flooding. Throughout Chinese history, great floods have struck the poor peasants trying to make their living from the land. This could be seen as an example of natural disasters, and these events are often reported as such in the media. Sartre is highly critical of the way in which these stories are told. He sees the Chinese floods as a consequence of the landscape and, specifically, the lack of trees to hold the land together, to create resistance against the waters.

The landscape has been made that way by hundreds of generations of farmers. In cutting down the trees, they have made far worse the dangers of flooding posed by the tides and the climate. Yet these events seem to them to be coming from outside:

> If some enemy of mankind had wanted to persecute the peasants of the great plain, he would have ordered mercenary troops to deforest the mountains systematically.

The floods are an example of a wider phenomenon: the way people experience the consequences of their own actions as acts of fate. Through Sartre's earlier thought there runs the theme of stolen consequences, as when Mathieu talks of all his actions having been stolen from him. These floods are a giant example of people losing contact with the consequences of their actions.

Sartre uses his favourite term 'negation' to define this situation. The past actions of the peasants are present as 'the absence of trees', that is as a negation, a lack which is every bit as real as all the presences in the world, as the rocks or the gulleys or the poor houses waiting to be swept away. The absence of trees is just as 'material' as the presence of water. The treeless slopes are also a negation in a more sinister sense: they are waiting to destroy the future, to annul the lives of the struggling people.

In the second example, city air fills with the smoke of the great factories. No one is immune to this terrible pollution which poisons the owners and their children along with the workers. Sartre calls this pollution a 'counter finality' for the employers. By this he means that the fumes have come about as a direct consequence of their actions, and yet consistently deny them the fulfilment of their aims, the good life which they seek so ruthlessly for themselves. Sartre sees many environmental and economic 'problems' as counter finalities. The ruling class pursues plans which have results that run counter to their own desires. Like negation, counter finality is a good example of dialectical method being applied to a specific issue. There is a conscious aim, and set against it there is an involuntary effect. The outcome is the new situation which is experienced as a 'problem'.

Prague, 1968: The Future of Revolution

SARTRE IN THE 1960s

Sartre became a key figure in the making of post-war Europe, as well as an iconic figure of the 1960s, the decade of rising youth dissent throughout the western world, of dissidence within the Soviet bloc and of the American involvement in the war in Vietnam. The year of 1968 saw the uprisings towards which the decade had pointed and takes its place in European revolutionary history with 1848, another moment of heroic defeats and lost possibilities, or of foolish dreams and iron reality.

Thinking of Sartre in the 1960s, one image stands out: the elderly and almost frail figure walking behind a protest placard at a massive Paris demonstration in May 1968. As we noted in the first chapter, Sartre was a direct influence upon the leaders of the student movement which was the would-be vanguard of uprising in Paris. But the year was more than the Paris episode, and after De Gaulle re-established official order in France, there were still other stories being played out elsewhere. One of the most important was in Czechoslovakia, and it is the Czech capital Prague which provides the key place and time for this chapter, for it was here that Sartre developed some of his richest responses to that year of lost ideals.

KEY MOMENT: PRAGUE, 1968

In the spring of 1968, the Czechoslovak regime led by Alexander Dubcek attempted to create a new type of socialist society, and to break the grip of the Soviet model on the Eastern bloc. The period known as the 'Prague spring' seemed to promise a new future for socialism. In retrospect, this Czech experiment quickly became the central symbol of that year. Soon after, in August 1968, the Soviet tanks put an end to this hope, as they had to the Hungarian attempt which had started Sartre on his search for a new political philosophy in 1956.

Sartre was quick and unambiguous in his condemnation of the Soviet invasion. He visited Prague from 28 November to 1 December 1969, and declared that the Czechs might still not have been finally defeated, despite the replacement of the more liberal regime by an orthodox Party machine. Sartre defined the meanings of Prague 1968 in an essay of 1969, which appeared in 1970 as 'The Socialism that came in from the Cold'. It compressed much of his critical thinking about Marxism and revolution.

Sartre saw the events of Prague in 1968 as raising the crucial question for the future of humanity. For him, the problem was to redeem the whole idea of revolutionary politics, and of socialism, from the corrupted form they had taken in the post-war world. Although he by no means dismissed what he saw as the positive achievements of the Soviet Union, in the end he asked what could be done:

> to prevent the next revolution from giving birth to that kind of socialism?

Sartre remained convinced that Marxist theory had a potential for being re-thought and that socialist society had the potential for being reborn, beyond the limits and corruptions of the Soviet system.

The struggle in Prague was, for Sartre, a sign that socialism had this promise which had not yet been fulfilled. The Czech regime had been able to make itself into the expression of a 'great popular movement', as opposed to the frozen state-dominated socialism of the Soviet bloc. From Sartre's point of view, Prague in 1968 was the place where 'the intellectuals recognized the radicalisation of their ideas'. In other words, ideas do not, in the end, find their full expression in the arguments or theories of thinkers, but in the lives and actions of people who respond to them in the world. In Sartre's version, the Czech intellectuals then took the opportunity 'and, at once, radicalized themselves'.

Sartre saw Prague as the temporary return of truth into the field of Marxist thinking, and this made it an occasion of historic importance, although the immediate defeat was inevitable. Certain intellectuals had begun to develop new ideas about socialism, and these ideas had been taken on by the movement of the people. This movement then made it possible for the thinkers to understand their own ideas better. In this model, truth is not a fixed definition, but a process of unfolding. He had put this idea in more philosophical terms in his work *The Search for a Method* from 1960:

> For us, truth is something which becomes, it *has* and *will have* become.

The 'us' in this declaration were Existentialists, and it remained Sartre's aim to revive Marxism by renewing its sense of this Existential truth. He had denounced 'frozen Marxism' in the name of this moving and changing truth, and he still hoped after 1968 to see the birth of a different revolutionary socialism which would acknowledge this Existential principle, while preserving other socialist ideas.

Prague marked the renewal of this sense of *Existential truth* in a socialist society. The intellectuals rejected, he felt, the old fixed system of thought, and embarked instead upon an experiment. In the old Marxism, theory was applied to the world. Nothing new emerged: it was simply a case of confirming what you already knew. If anything did not fit, it must be eliminated in the name of the theory. But in Prague new version, truth was in the future. Ideas were just beginning their search. In *Search for a Method* Sartre had declared firmly that:

> Far from being exhausted, Marxism is still very young, almost in its infancy; it has scarcely begun to develop.

Prague now stood concretely for this hope, the hope that Marxism could still grow far beyond its current and previous forms.

When we think now of the Soviet system, what comes to mind is a huge exercise in censorship. Nothing could be allowed to exist if it did not conform to the theory. Sartre had already diagnosed this as the essential 'problem of Stalinism', but he always insisted that Marxism had the potential to outlive this phase of frozen dogma. In the history of the struggle against Soviet censorship, we tend now to remember the individual dissident thinkers, writers or artists. In Prague, Sartre felt a whole society coming to the defence of the dissident demand for freedom of thought:

> But what is striking for someone from the West is that the battle of the intellectuals for complete freedom of expression and information was supported by the workers.

Prague represented the possibility of socialism without censorship. On the contrary, in this new society 'total truth was an absolute necessity' for all. This was because everyone was involved in making the decisions as to how their enterprises should run, and no one could make such decisions if they did not have the facts. In the Soviet model, the leaders already know the truth, and if anything does not fit, it must be suppressed. The economy must illustrate the plan. In the Prague alternative, no one can know the truth in advance. History does not illustrate pre-given truths, it re-makes ideas in the light of new events and actions.

Sartre described the Soviet invasion as precisely an assault by frozen Marxism on socialist development:

> ...the leaders of the USSR, appalled at seeing socialism once more on the move, sent their tanks to Prague to stop it.

The key phrase here is 'on the move'. Prague represents the socialism whose ideas are still 'becoming'; the USSR embodies the socialism whose idea is already finalized. This is a struggle between two radically opposed philosophies of truth and history, each with a claim to represent socialism.

Concept File: Marxism

Old Stalinism	New Revolution
History is destiny.	History includes choice and chance.
The Party re-makes society from above.	Local decision-making enabled by a wider system (workers' councils).
Censorship.	Universal information.

SARTRE'S MARXISM

The history of the Soviet bloc is dominated by those two invasions – the 1968 moment when the tanks rolled into Prague spring and the 1956 moment when the tanks crushed the Hungarian uprising. Sartre began his critique of 'frozen Marxism' in response to the Hungarian episode, and it was these ideas which informed his view of the Czech defeat. Let us look now at the wider significance of his total attack on mainstream Soviet Marxism, an attack which still has implications for the future in the twenty-first century.

Sartre anticipated the failure of the Soviet model and was already attempting to develop an alternative within Marxist thought. It is worth pausing over this attempt, not only to see it in its context, but to ask whether it still has anything to offer now. The key work in which Sartre explored the problem of orthodox Marxism or Stalinism was the tellingly entitled *The Search for a Method*, published as a preliminary part of the larger *Critique*. A *Search* is a fitting place to end this account of Sartre's writing and thought in their times.

The book opens with an exciting and dramatic account of Marxism and Existentialism, which is one of the most important texts in the history of twentieth-century political philosophy. For a while, it seems as if Sartre is going to tell a story in which he started off as an Existentialist and then grew up and became a Marxist. He declares firmly that in the second half of the twentieth century there is no 'going beyond' Marxist philosophy. Anyone who claims to see further than Marxism is merely falling back into an earlier and outmoded theory. This looks like a solid commitment. But by the start of the second section, Sartre is asking the question:

Why then, are we not simply Marxists?

It turns out that the 'us' is still Existentialists, and what keeps them from being 'simply' Marxists is that it is not possible for an Existentialist to believe that the truth is already known; any system which claims to possess the final truth is bound to be self-defeating.

Marxism, for Sartre, was in possession of some really fundamental principles, particularly concerning human history. He was convinced that there is an economic basis to the way in which history unfolds, and that Marxism in many ways does have the key to understanding how human choices are shaped. Nevertheless, Sartre saw Marxism as having lost track of its own principles. He gives as an example the case of the French Revolution. Marxism says that the political events have a basis in the conflict between classes and, particularly, between the rising power of the bourgeoisie, the old aristocracy and the working people. Sartre warns that this approach which explains everything in terms of class conflict 'causes those men whom we know well to disappear'. Individuals are eliminated from history, leaving only an abstract explanation. Yet as Sartre insists, talking about a political group that held power in the revolution, 'the Girondists *existed*'.

In his later political thought as in his earlier fiction, Sartre confronts us with existence. He warns that there are no systems which will enable us to rise above the world of individual people and things. Even the most convincing theory, which he takes Marxism to be, cannot ever ignore the 'men whom we know', the fact that certain people existed. Sartre uses this example to denounce the orthodox Marxists:

This lazy Marxism puts everything into everything, makes real men into the symbols of its myths.

Sartre demands that Marxism accept the limitations of its theories, of *all* theories in the face of this *existence*.

The Idea of Sartre

12

In her autobiography of the 1930s and the war years, Simone de Beauvoir creates a classic image of intellectual life, commitment to ideas even at the limits of everyday survival. Sartre has just returned from the Prisoner of War camp; the Nazis rule Paris; challenging graffiti are, at the time, all that express Parisian defiance of their occupiers: the V-sign, the English symbol of victory, began to appear in chalk and paint all over Paris'. Sartre has helped found a resistance group; notices of warning and execution appear on the same walls as the victory signs:

> Sartre had settled down to work again. Before sitting down to write the philosophical opus [*Being and Nothingness*] he had planned, bit by bit, during his time in Alsace, and latterly in the Stalag, he decided to finish off *The Age of Reason*.
>
> *The Prime of Life*, de Beauvoir

Ideas are not an alternative to experience or even action: but finally, there is this overriding passion for thought, and the writing of thoughts.

Having pursued ideas uncompromisingly throughout his life and times, Jean-Paul Sartre has become an idea. Of course, the idea means different things to different people; there are as many interpretations of Sartre as there are interpreters. But he has become one of the great representatives of what it meant to be 'an intellectual' in the twentieth century, and what it might mean in the twenty-first century.

The idea of Sartre bursts through in the memoir of his pupil, and later friend, J.B. Pontalis, who became an eminent psychoanalyst and writer. Writing in the 1980s, Pontalis recalls Sartre as a teacher in 1941:

With Sartre – for he it was – (the outstanding, trenchant man), everything totally altered.

This is the intellectual as educator, and even saviour. With touches of irony, the pupil still conjures up the impact of Sartre at that moment when he was in the midst of his most productive period as a writer. In the context of the occupation, Sartre stood for intellectual hope, and integrity. On the one hand, the world was never to be simplified, not to be confused with our reactions or theories. On the other hand, we could aspire to some understanding of this alien presence, we could hope to make our own sense of things:

Nothing was assimilable but everything was intelligible.

This Sartre is a thinker whose thoughts are responses to the immediate world, the impact of specific things and people:

When Sartre took the metro, I imagined that he asked himself the question: 'What exactly is the metro?' – the damp heat, or a tired face? – just so as not to stop thinking.

Sartre is the idea of thinking in the world. His ideas are hooked on to things; they offer no escape from experience. Instead, this is a thinker whose thoughts plunge back into life, when so many other philosophers and writers have promised to rise above the mundane world, to transcend the common limits. Sartre is the thinker of our own limits, the voice of things.

For Iris Murdoch in 1953, Sartre took upon himself with integrity a common situation:

> As a European socialist intellectual with an acute sense of the needs of his time, Sartre wishes to affirm the preciousness of the individual and the possibility of a society which is free and democratic ... This affirmation is his most profound concern and the key to all his thought...

Here, too, the idea of Sartre is bound up with hope in dark times. For Murdoch, Sartre is the intellectual who remains true to the task of affirmation, in the face of the most acute awareness of contradictions and dangers. He works his way through almost every negative concept that one could imagine, not for its own sake, but in order to rescue all the more convincingly the prospect for a future affirmation, or even re-affirmation. Sartre sees only too clearly the extreme isolation of the individual in practice, an isolation that Murdoch terms 'solipsistic', turned in on itself. But he wants to make a way back towards the light of a common world:

> The individual is the centre, but a solipsistic centre. He has a *dream* of human companionship, but never the experience ... The best he can attain to is an intuition of paradise...

Murdoch sees in Sartre a 'non-Christian thinker', one who will refuse the old certainties without lapsing into cynicism, on the one hand, or settling for new certainties on the other hand.

For the eminent literary theorist, Frederic Jameson, at the start of his career in 1961, Sartre was the writer who called on us to re-think our whole language. He confronts the reader with:

> the simple opposition … between consciousness and things … this radical difference in being.

We like to think of our words as fitting neatly over the world of things. Sartre demands that we go back to the start, and in a new spirit 'check all our ideas … all our formulations.' Nothing is to be taken as read, yet Sartre, unlike later theorists, retains a hope that we will be able to bridge, at times, the gap between our consciousness and the world of things in which we live. Once again, the idea of Sartre is bound up with an intellectual hope. Sartre summons us, his readers, to participate in:

> this struggle of unique qualities against the names that both fix them and make them too general…

Normally, one thinks of the intellect as a means of generalizing from experience, or rising beyond its limitations, but for Jameson, Sartre represents an intellectual pathway which leads back to the world of particular things and unique experiences.

The literary critic Dennis Hollier, writing in 1982, celebrates Sartre's attachments to particular times and dates. He recounts his own experience of the news of Sartre's death precisely in the manner of Sartre himself, in, for instance, *The Reprieve*:

> BERKELEY 15 April 1980. 7.p.m. Pacific Time. Tuesday, I believe. The evening news announces that '"French philosopher Jean-Paul Sartre is dead."

In death, Sartre the philosopher belongs still to the world of specific times and places. Hollier is trying to re-create for us an idea of Sartre, as the philosopher of the specific instant, in experience and history.

In the end, though, we must return to Sartre's own idea of himself and his work, as expressed in his post-war literary manifesto:

> A bare tear is not lovely. It offends. A good argument also offends ... But an argument that masks a tear – that's what we're after.
>
> *What Is Writing?* (or *What is Literature*), 1947

Sartre is a writer of good arguments, even great arguments, as we have seen: in novels, in plays, in essays, in philosophical systems. But his arguments are always poised on the edge of this 'tear', this emotion which he expresses so much more vividly by concealment. Sartre is an idea, but he is also a feeling about ideas.

Further Reading

Works by Jean-Paul Sartre

The following are works which have been directly discussed, given in the editions cited and quoted:

Anti-Semite and Jew, trans. George J. Becker, Schocken Books, 1995.

Baudelaire, trans. Martin Turnell, New Directions, 1950.

Being and Nothingness, trans. Hazel E. Barnes, Routledge, 1958.

The Critique of Dialectical Reason, trans. Alan Sheridan-Smith, Verso, 1976.

In Camera (or *No Exit*), trans. Stuart Gilbert, in *In Camera and Other Plays*, Penguin, 1990.

Iron in the Soul, trans. Gerard Hopkins, Penguin, 1985.

Modern Times: Selected Non-Fiction [for essays on Paris, world cities, Prague spring], trans. Robin Buss and editied by Geoffrey Wall, Penguin, 2000.

Nausea, trans. Robert Baldick, Penguin, 1965.

The Age of Reason, trans. Eric Sutton, Penguin, 1986.

'The Humanism of Existentialism', trans. Bernard Frechtman in *Essays in Existentialism*, Citadel Press, 1993.

Search for a Method, trans. Hazel E. Barnes, Vintage Books, 1968.

The Psychology of the Imagination, intro. Mary Warnock, Routledge, 1972.

The Reprieve, trans. Eric Sutton, Penguin, 1986.

War Diaries, trans. Quintin Hoare, Verso, 1999.

'*What is Writing?*', [orig. '*What is Literature?*', trans. Bernard Frechtman in *Essays in Existentialism*, Citadel Press, 1993.

Words, trans. Irene Clephane, Penguin, 1967.

Works on Jean-Paul Sartre
The following is a selection of varied and significant works, including those cited in the text:

Barnes, H.E., *Sartre*. Quartet Books, 1974.
Catalano, J.S., *A Commentary on Jean-Paul Sartre's 'Being and Nothingness'*. University of Chicago Press, 1980.
Caute, D., *The Fellow Travellers*. Quartet, 1977.
Danto, A., *Sartre*. Fontana, 1975.
Dobson, A., *Jean-Paul Sartre and the Politics of Reason*. Cambridge University Press, 1993.
Fulbook, K. and Fulbrook, E., *Simone de Beauvoir and Jean-Paul Sartre*. Harvester, 1993.
Gerassi, J. *Jean-Paul Sartre: Hated Conscience of His Century*. University of Chicago Press, 1989.
Hayman, R., *Writing Against: A Biography of Sartre*. Weidenfeld and Nicolson, 1986.
Hollier, D., *The Politics of Prose: Essay on Sartre*, trans. Jeffrey Mehlman, Minnesota University Press, 1986.
Howells, C. (ed), *The Cambridge Companion to Sartre*. Cambridge University Press, 1992.
Jameson, F., Sartre: *The Origins of a Style*. Yale University Press, 1961.
McCulloch, G., *Using Sartre*. Routledge, 1994.
Merleau-Ponty, M., *Sense and Non-Sense*, trans. Hubert L. Dreyfus and Patricia Allen Dreyfus. Northwestern University Press, 1964.
Murdoch, I., *Sartre: Romantic Rationalist*. Penguin, 1989; orig. 1953.
Pontalis, J.B., *Love of Beginnings*, trans. James Greene and Marie-Christine Réguis. Free Association Books, 1993.
Warnock, M., *The Philosophy of Sartre*. Hutchinson, 1965.

Other Works Cited
de Beauvoir, S., *The Prime of Life*, trans. Peter Green. Andre Deutsch and Weidenfeld and Nicolson, 1962.
Heidegger, M., *Being and Time*, trans. J.Macquarrie and E.Robinson. Blackwell, 1962.

INDEX

BUDDHA –
A BEGINNER'S GUIDE

Gillian Stokes

Buddha – A Beginner's Guide introduces you to the Buddha, whose exemplary life and teaching has inspired one of the greatest world faiths.

Gillian Stokes's informative text explores:

- the Buddha's background and the times he lived in
- the legends surrounding this inspirational teacher
- the key teachings and concepts of the Buddhist tradition
- the role of Buddhism in the world today.

The facts … the concepts … the ideas …

GANDHI –
A BEGINNER'S GUIDE

Genevieve Blais

Gandhi – A Beginner's Guide invites you to take a glimpse into the life of this profound character. Follow his extraordinary quest for morality, justice and spirituality and discover how his strategy of passive resistance achieved social reform. Find out how his influence has now extended far beyond the barriers of a nation.

Genevieve Blais's compelling text investigates:

- Gandhi's background and the times he lived in
- Britain's role in the history of India
- the events leading up to and prior to the Salt March
- Gandhi's role in the independence of India
- his assassination and legacy.

The facts … the concepts … the ideas …

CHARLES DARWIN – A BEGINNER'S GUIDE

Gill Hands

Charles Darwin – A Beginner's Guide introduces you to the man whose scientific observations on evolution challenged the religious beliefs of Victorian society, but which are now generally accepted as being perfectly logical. Examine the historical perspective of evolution and the various philosophical questions that arise. No need to wrestle with difficult concepts as key ideas are presented in a clear jargon-free way.

Gill Hands' informative text explores:

- Darwin's background the times he lived in
- the development of the theory of natural selection
- the scientific basis for evolution
- the relevance of his ideas in today's world.

The facts … the concepts … the ideas …

ISAAC NEWTON – A BEGINNER'S GUIDE

Jane Jakeman

Isaac Newton – A Beginner's Guide introduces you to the towering genius. Explore how his science revolutionized our world and his philosophy changed our thought. Find out more about Newton the man, and as scientist, philosopher, alchemist and respected public figure.

Jane Jakeman's lively text;

- describes Newton's background and the times he lived in
- explores his scientific ideas and their effect on our lives
- delves into the character of the man
- examines the influence of Newton on his own time and today.

The facts … the concepts … the ideas …

LOUIS PASTEUR – A BEGINNER'S GUIDE

Peter Gosling

Louis Pasteur – A Beginner's Guide introduces you to the life and work of one of the greatest scientists of the nineteenth century. Find out how his discoveries in chemistry, bacteriology and medicine opened up new fields of research, and discover more about the significance and number of accomplishments that have transformed Pasteur into a popular icon.

Peter Gosling's informative text explores:

- Pasteur's background and the times he lived in
- his role in the foundation of bacteriology
- his work on fermentation and pasteurisation
- the development of the germ theory of disease
- his instrumentation in the development of vaccines
- the relevance of his ideas in today's world.

The facts … the concepts … the ideas …

JUNG –
A BEGINNER'S GUIDE

Ruth Berry

Jung – A Beginner's Guide gives you the essential facts and concepts behind the 'father of analytical psychology' and his work. No need to wrestle with difficult concepts as key ideas are presented in a clear and jargon-free way.

Ruth Berry's lively text takes you step-by-step through:

- Jung's background and the times he lived in
- the development of Jungian analysis in simple terms and the key concepts and ideas surrounding his work
- the study of dreams and their interpretation
- the archetypal interpretation of popular myths and legends
- the concept of the symbol

The facts … the concepts … the ideas …

DA VINCI –
A BEGINNER'S GUIDE

Ruth Berry

Da Vinci – A Beginner's Guide introduces you to the life and work of a great genius. Leonardo is usually thought of as an artist, but he was also an intellectual giant in the developing field of science and an accomplished musician, architect and engineer. Follow the story of a true genius rich in ideas.

Ruth Berry's lively text investigates:

- ■ Leonardo's background and the times he lived in
- ■ The importance of the Renaissance
- ■ Leonardo's influence on the world of art
- ■ His astounding explorations in science and technology.

The facts … the concepts … the ideas …

MARX –
A BEGINNER'S GUIDE

Gill Hands

Marx – A Beginner's Guide gives you the essential facts surrounding the 'father of communism'. No need to wrestle with difficult concepts as key themes and ideas are presented in a clear and jargon-free way.

Gill Hand's no-nonsense text takes you step-by-step through:

- Marx's background and the times he lived in
- the ideas that led to revolutions throughout the world
- the place of Marxism and Marx
- Marx's world outlook.

The facts ... the concepts ... the ideas ...

EINSTEIN –
A BEGINNER'S GUIDE

Jim Breithaupt

Einstein – A Beginner's Guide introduces you to the great scientist and his work. No need to wrestle with difficult concepts as key ideas are presented in a clear and jargon-free way.

Jim Breithaupt's lively text:

- presents Einstein's work in historical context
- sets out the experimental evidence in support of Einstein's theories
- takes you through the theory of relativity, in simle terms
- describes the predictions from Einstein's theories on the future of the universe.

The facts … the concepts … the ideas …